Cultural Heritage and Contemporary Change
Series IVA. Eastern and Central European Philosophical Studies, Volume 51
Series VIII. Christian Philosophical Studies, Volume 10
General Editor
George F. McLean

A Czech Perspective on Faith in a Secular Age

Czech Philosophical Studies, V
Christian Philosophical Studies, X

Edited by
Tomáš Halík
Pavel Hošek

The Council for Research in Values and Philosophy

Copyright © 2015 by

The Council for Research in Values and Philosophy

Box 261
Cardinal Station
Washington, D.C. 20064

All rights reserved

Printed in the United States of America

Library of Congress Cataloging-in-Publication

A Czech perspective on faith in a secular age / edited by Tomáš Halík, Pavel Hošek. -- first edition.

pages cm. -- (Cultural heritage and contemporary change. Series IVA, Eastern and Central European philosophical studies ; Volume 51) (Cultural heritage and contemporary change. Series VIII, Christian philosophical studies ; Volume 10) (Czech philosophical studies ; V)

Includes bibliographical references and index.

1. Catholic Church--Czech Republic. 2. Christianity and atheism. 3. Czech Republic--Religion. 4. Secularism--Czech Republic. I. Halík, Tomáš, editor.

BX1527.3.C94 2015   2014041773
282'.4371--dc23   CIP

ISBN 978-1-56518-300-1 (pbk)

TABLE OF CONTENTS

Introduction: Towards a Kenotic Hermeneutics of   1
Contemporary Czech Culture
   Pavel Hošek

Chapter I. Discerning the Signs of the Times in Post-communist   13
Czech Republic: A Historical, Sociological and Missiological
Analysis of Contemporary Czech Culture
   Pavel Hošek

Chapter II. The Catholic Church and Czech Society before   43
and after the Fall of Communism
   Tomáš Halík

Chapter III. Europe between Laicity and Christianity   53
   Tomáš Halík

Chapter IV. "The Myth of the 'Nonreligious Age'":   61
A Sociocultural Transformation of Religion in Modernity
   Pavel Roubík

Chapter V. A Postmodern Quest: Seeking God and Religious   81
Language in a Postmodern Context
   Martin Kočí

Chapter VI. Searching the Altar of an Unknown God: 95
Tomáš Halík on Faith in a Secular Age
   Martin Kočí and Pavel Roubík

Chapter VII. Church for the Seekers   125
   Tomáš Halík

About the Authors   133
Index   135

INTRODUCTION

TOWARDS A KENOTIC HERMENEUTICS OF CONTEMPORARY CZECH CULTURE

PAVEL HOŠEK

Religious faith is going through an unprecedented transformation in the contemporary world. One of the major causes of this transformation is the fact that we are living in "a secular age", to use the phrase chosen as a title of the now famous book by Charles Taylor. Traditional religious institutions do not seem to be very quick in adjusting their programs and ways of communication to the contemporary cultural situation. This volume is one of the outcomes of an international research project entitled "Faith in a Secular Age", whose goal is to help the contemporary Church to understand better what is going on with religious faith in contemporary societies and to adapt its pastoral activities and methods to changing cultural conditions.

The book was written by four theologians. It is a result of long-term team work, which consisted of a series of meetings, dialogue sessions, debates and informal conversations and countless e-mails and phone calls among the four team members: Tomáš Halík, the inofficial guru of the group, and three of his younger friends and disciples, Pavel Hošek, Martin Kočí and Pavel Roubík. All are students and teachers of theology deeply interested in contemporary sociology of religion, just like their master.

All four read and discussed together with great enthusiasm and approval Charles Taylor's ground breaking book *A Secular Age*[1] and tried to test and apply its insights and interpretive suggestions on the strangely unique situation of the Czech Republic.

Czech society is in many respects a test case and a "laboratory" of secularizing trends and their inner dynamics[2]. It is one of the most secular societies in the world. What makes Czech secularity quite interesting is the fact that it does not consist of widely held atheist convictions or materialist philosophy or complete spiritual indifference.

---

[1] Charles Taylor, *A Secular Age* (Cambridge, MT: Harvard University Press, 2007).

[2] Cf. Petr Fiala, *The Laboratory of Secularisation: Religion and Politics in a Non-religious Society: the Czech Case (Laboratoř sekularizace. Náboženství a politika v ne-náboženské společnosti: český příklad)* (Brno: CDK, 2007).

Czech people are generally quite interested in non-materialist interpretations of reality and they are in fact far above average in their interest in alternative spiritualities[3]. In other words, most Czechs are in fact "seekers" of one sort or another, yet very few are "dwellers".

Czech secularity is, as local sociological research projects clearly show, specifically anti-ecclesial or anti-clerical. Czechs generally speaking feel an a priori distrust towards institutionalized and organized religion. Czech believers are therefore in a unique situation. They are a small minority, surrounded by a secular majority. So their experience with the effective (and also ineffective) ways of evangelization and reaching out to contemporary seekers may perhaps be useful for other Christians, facing similar conditions or struggling with gradual changes of general attitudes towards the Church similar to those typical of the Czech situation. Some European countries may well be going through earlier stages of the process which has brought about the contemporary state of affairs in the Czech Republic.

At the same time of course, since the Czech situation is in some respects exceptional and unique (perhaps comparable to the situation in Estonia and Eastern Germany), it may imply some limitations concerning the applicability of the specifically Czech experience in other contexts. In other words, the Czech situation is a result of a long and complex series of particular historical, cultural and political events, trends and influences, a very unique series, indeed.

This is why, for example, all the neighbouring countries (Germany, Austria, Poland, Slovakia) show dramatically different results in sociological research related to general attitudes towards faith, spirituality, religion, Church etc. All the neighbouring countries have one thing in common: a much higher (in fact in all cases *several times* higher) percentage of people with a positive/affirmative attitude to religious faith and belong (at least nominally) to a church.

In the Czech situation, it is probably more obvious than anywhere else that if the Church wants to speak to contemporary people in an intelligible way, it has to follow Charles Taylor's advice and move from the traditional believers – nonbelievers paradigm to the more illuminating and adequate seekers – dwellers paradigm. Believers and nonbelievers do not seem to be two strictly separated groups, definitely not in contemporary Czech society. A typical contemporary Czech

---

[3] Dana Hamplová, *Religion in Czech Society on the Treshhold of the Third Millenium* (*Náboženství v české společnosti na prahu třetího tisíciletí*) (Praha: Karolinum, 2013), p. 69ff.

person is often "simul fidelis et infidelis"[4]. The number of those who fully identify themselves with the teaching and practice of institutional Church is very small and obviously continues to decrease[5]. The indefinite grey zone between traditional believers and convinced atheists keeps growing. The key question for today seems to be: what are the appropriate ways the Church should understand and respond to the needs and questions of contemporary seekers?[6] The grey zone is in fact very diverse and multifarious. It includes "apatheists" (those who are basically indifferent towards religion), it also includes those who are attracted by various kinds of new spiritual options such as Westernized versions of Eastern religious traditions or esoteric spiritualities. Among both regular and less regular Church-goers (who may be more or less loyal Church members though perhaps not completely satisfied with its contemporary shape) and also among people who call themselves "spiritual but not religious", and even among those who are radical critics of contemporary Christianity and call themselves atheists, we find many sincere seekers.

An alternative way of speaking about seekers and dwellers is (as T. Halík suggests) to distinguish between *open-minded* and *closed–minded* people. The former remain open to Mystery, Love, and Hope. The latter sometimes prefer to have things, including spiritual things, "under control" (at the same time, we must remember that not all dwellers are necessarily closed-minded). The faith of seekers tends to be rather implicit and shy. This mode of faith happens to be quite typical for the Czech religious situation[7], as it becomes obvious when we look at some of the archetypal figures of the Czech political and cultural history (e.g. Karel Havlíček Borovský, Tomáš G. Masaryk, Karel Čapek, Václav Havel) – they were neither atheists, nor ordinary Church believers, but were definitely seekers[8].

Those who still focus on traditional believers and Church-goers tend to conclude that a society, where the number of people who identify with the Church is decreasing (which is definitely the case in the Czech

---

[4] Tomáš Halík. *I Want You to Be (Chci, abys byl)* (Praha: Lidové noviny, 2012), p. 20.

[5] Radek Tichý and Martin Vávra. *Religion from a Different Angle (Náboženství z jiného úhlu)* (Brno: CDK, 2012), p. 19ff.

[6] Tomáš Halík. *Near to Those who Are Distant (Vzdáleným nablízku)* (Praha: Lidové noviny, 2007), p. 38.

[7] Tomáš Halík. *Near to Those who Are Distant (Vzdáleným nablízku)* (Praha: Lidové noviny, 2007), p. 89ff.

[8] Tomáš Halík. *What Does not Shiver is not Firm (Co je bez chvění, není pevné)* (Praha: Lidové noviny, 2002), p. 210ff.

Republic), is therefore becoming more and more atheist. But this erroneous conclusion is based on understanding believers as "dwellers". Considering the situation from a particularly Czech perspective, it seems obvious that the Church should not function just as a safe home and shelter for dwellers. A significant step in this direction has been made by the proposals of the documents of the II Vatican council, seeking a new (less defensive and more balanced) understanding of secularity, secular humanism and modern atheism. It seems that the legacy of the II Vatican council may and in fact should lead to a transition from "Catholicism" to "catholicity"[9], a transition from "fortress-catholicism" as a "counterculture against modernity"[10] towards an open-minded catholic Christianity. This understands the ecclesial community of Christians as a "creative minority", operating in an ecumenical, dialogical and dynamic way[11]. Such transition would be, judging from a particularly Czech perspective, highly desirable.

Pope Benedict XVI proposed – during his visit in the Czech Republic in September 2009 – the idea of the "courtyard for the gentiles": the Church must not operate as an isolationist religious organisation, it should offer certain space for those who do not fully share its faith, i.e. for seekers. The idea that the Church must be in touch with people who do not profess Christianity and who perhaps just vaguely desire "something beyond", is very important and extremely relevant for the Czech cultural context. At the same time, a Czech Christian and especially a Czech seeker might find it difficult to resist the suspicion that behind the metaphor of the "courtyard for gentiles" there still operates a certain triumphalist understanding of the Church. That is why Czech theologians might want to rephrase the question and ask: Is the Church today really in the position of opening the "courtyard for gentiles" or is she rather sent out to humbly look for various "gentile courtyards" and to try to address the gentiles there – in their own language?[12]

This concern, based on the particularly Czech experience, is the driving force and motivation behind our team's attempt at a *kenotic hermeneutics of contemporary culture*, guided by the biblical metaphor

---

[9] Tomáš Halík. *Vocatus et Invocatus* (*Vzýván i nevzýván*) (Praha: Lidové noviny, 2004), p. 72.

[10] Tomáš Halík. *Vocatus et Invocatus* (*Vzýván i nevzýván*) (Praha: Lidové noviny, 2004), p. 215ff.

[11] Tomáš Halík. *Hope Remains for the Tree* (*Stromu zbývá naděje*) (Praha: Lidové noviny, 2009), p. 63.

[12] Tomáš Halík. *Spectacle for the Angels* (*Divadlo pro anděly*) (Praha: Lidové noviny, 2010), p. 140ff.

of "discerning the signs of the times"[13]. We strongly believe that no triumphalist proclamation of the Christian message accompanied by judgemental critique of contemporary culture is going to work.

What do we mean by a "kenotic hermeneutics of contemporary (Czech) culture", which has been the guiding perspective of all our team members? We strongly believe that the calling of the Church includes listening attentively to, and trying to understand, the actual questions people are asking, as they are articulated in one way or another in art, in philosophy, in the climate of society, in changes of public opinion, in media, and so on. This means being well versed in contemporary culture and its artistic and philosophical reflection, and searching for ways to engage in a meaningful dialogue.

"Discerning the signs of the times" and searching for points at which to engage in an intelligible and mutually enriching conversation with contemporary culture in fact presupposes a certain "moderate optimism" in regard to contemporary people outside the Church. This moderate optimism does not forget the darker side of biblical and ecclesial teaching about human nature. At the same time it humbly and attentively watches for "rays of eternal truth, beauty, and good" in general (secular) culture, elements which can be recognised and appreciated on the part of Christians and can become the starting-point for dialogue. In the final analysis, European culture would be unthinkable without the influence of Christianity over the last two thousand years, and many values and ideals of the modern West can undoubtedly be viewed as "mature fruits of the Gospel".

In a dialogue like this between more traditional Christians and seekers the former can (if they are asked) testify to their faith and point to the transcendent source of those rays of eternal truth, beauty, and good in contemporary culture, i.e. to their "heavenly origin".

Everything that is good, truthful, and beautiful in contemporary culture can, and indeed should be considered by Christians as manifestations or fruits of universal divine revelation and universal grace that embraces all people, not just Christians. This is what the apostle Paul has in mind when he advises the Christians in Philippi: "Whatever is true, whatever is noble, whatever is right, whatever is pure, whatever is lovely, whatever is admirable – if anything is excellent or praiseworthy – think about such things"[14]. The meaning of this New Testament affirmation can certainly be interpreted as implying that many elements of general culture evidently have their origin in the fact that all

---

[13] Gospel of Matthew 16, 2-3.
[14] Letter to Philippians 4, 8.

people are created in God's image and in some way "reflect God's glory", whether consciously or not, whether with grateful affirmation or quite without any conscious relationship to the Creator and Giver of life.

Within the framework of this essentially favourable prospect it is then possible to welcome many characteristic features of contemporary (Czech) culture and affirm them, because in fact they often reflect profound truths that were always part of the biblical tradition and were or should have been an integral part of Christian faith. It is true that some of them may have been partially forgotten, suppressed, or marginalised in the history of Christianity, so that in fact it is the contemporary culture that reminds Christians of them again. In this sense contemporary culture may be an opportunity for some partially forgotten elements of the Christian tradition to be heard again at full strength. In fact, it is an opportunity *for Christians themselves* to rediscover these elements, to proclaim their adherence to them once again.

This is not a case of rash and hasty "adapting to the spirit of the times". It just seems obvious that contemporary culture is cultivating some values that should be proclaimed and cultivated by the Church, and (in some cases) this has not been the case because the Church has either forgotten these values or betrayed them. Change on the side of the Church is therefore not out of place and it is not a question of "selling off the family silver" or courting the popularity of "spoilt contemporaries".

This approach to culture is theologically justified by the traditional understanding of the role of the Church as the "continuation of Christ's incarnation", admittedly with a strong kenotic emphasis.[15] Just as the Word became flesh and dwelt among people[16], so Christians should "dwell among people", and not in the safety of a religious ghetto or ecclesial subculture. Just as Christ, who although "being in very nature God, did not consider equality with God a thing to be grasped, but made himself nothing, taking the very nature of a servant, being made in human likeness"[17], so Christians should follow his example and not remain in the shelter of their Church subculture, but „make themselves nothing" and "take on the nature of a servant", in other words learn to understand contemporary people and speak their language. Just as Christ took on human nature, because "what is not accepted, cannot be redeemed", so Christians today should "take on" the questions,

---

[15] Tomáš Halík. *I Want You to Be* (*Chci, abys byl*) (Praha: Lidové noviny, 2012), p. 141ff, 220ff.

[16] Gospel of John 1, 14.

[17] Letter to Philippians 2, 6f.

challenges, and uncertainties of their contemporaries. Why? Because what is not accepted, cannot be redeemed[18].

A similar conclusion can be drawn from an attentive examination of Jesus's teaching in the Gospels: Jesus did not speak the language of exalted theology or the language of angels. He spoke the language of the people among whom he was sent. His parables relate to the daily reality of Galilean farmers and craftsmen. If Christians today, in an attempt to be faithful to the Bible and tradition, speak to their contemporaries about fishing in the Sea of Galilee, the wedding-feast at Cana, or the sower of wheat seed, they will achieve more or less exactly the opposite effect. In order for Christians to know what corresponds to fishing, the wedding-feast at Cana, and sowing grain in the thought of people today, in other words in order for them to learn how they are to pass on the content of Jesus's teaching and which "parables of the Kingdom of God" they need to tell *today*, they have to plunge deeply into the coordinates of contemporary culture, otherwise their message will be condemned to being incomprehensible.

The same lesson can be learned from the well-known statement by the apostle Paul, when he summed up his missiological "communication strategy" as follows: "To the Jews I became like a Jew, to win the Jews. To those under the law I became like one under the law..., so as to win those under the law. To those not having the law I became like one not having the law..., so as to win those not having the law. To the weak I became weak, to win the weak."[19] Today he would probably add: To those who are seeking I became seeking.... This is (in a nutshell) the theological perspective that lies behind the essays collected in this book.

The first two chapters have a historical and regional focus: In the first chapter entitled "**Discerning the Signs of the Times in Post-communist Czech Republic**" Pavel Hošek deals with the most influential theories explaining the historical and sociological causes of Czech secularity, and shortly describes the gradually changing relationship between the majority of Czech society and the Church over the last two centuries. He also discusses some of the proposed explanations for the exceptionally high distrust towards the Church in the Czech context, accompanied, interestingly, by a growing and generally very high degree of interest in alternative spiritualities. In the following part of the first chapter, a missiological hermeneutics of

---

[18] Tomáš Halík. *Vocatus et Invocatus* (*Vzýván i nevzýván*) (Praha: Lidové noviny, 2004), p. 179.
[19] First Letter to Corinthians 9, 20-22.

contemporary cultural trends is proposed. In subsequent paragraphs, several key features of contemporary Czech culture are briefly discussed and missiological implications suggested, namely the post-rationalist, post-ideological, post-traditional, post-optimistic, post-individualist and post-materialist aspects of contemporary culture.

In the second chapter entitled "**Catholic Church and the Czech Society before and after the Fall of Communism**" Tomáš Halík summarizes recent history of the Roman Catholic Church in Czechoslovakia before and after the Velvet revolution in 1989, which brought about the fall of the communist totalitarian regime. He analyzes the most important social and cultural transformations over the last several decades and pays special attention to how the Church has been perceived by secular society and how it responded or failed to respond to the changing cultural situation in the post-communist Czech Republic.

The next two chapters focus on the nature of secularity and its relation to Christianity: In the third chapter, entitled "**Europe between Laicity and Christianity**" Tomáš Halík focuses on the complex history of European Christianity in relation to its "sibling" secularity. He offers a theological interpretation of secularity as a "Christian" phenomenon and distinguishes it strictly form the ambitious and quasi-religious ideology of secularism. If secularity or secular humanism does not degenerate into secularism, and if, at the same time, Christianity does not degenerate into defensive religious fundamentalism, both secularity and Christianity may become key creative cultural forces of the future, co-existing in an interactive and mutually enriching way, correcting each other's onesidedness and engaging each other in a fruitful dialogue.

In the fourth chapter entitled "**'The Myth of the <Nonreligious Age>': A Sociocultural Transformation of Religion in Modernity**" Pavel Roubík focuses on the transformation of religion since the Enlightenment. In the first part of his chapter, he deals with the sociological models of secularization and their limits. In the second part he focuses on the question of the relationship between secularization and the Enlightenment, and in the third part, which is the most important one, he tries to analyse the crisis of religion employing the very notion of secularization as a hermeneutical category, focusing on the following features of contemporary culture: bureaucracy, capitalism, technology, democratization, media and loss of gratitude.

The next two chapters focus on philosophical and theological interpretations of postmodernity as they may be used in discussing the most positive and appropriate responses of the Church to the changing cultural conditions today and in the future.

In the fifth chapter entitled "**A Postmodern Quest: Seeking God and Religious Language in a Postmodern Context**" Martin Kočí explores the identity of contemporary seekers and defines them as the *people of questions*. The author deals with the following questions: Which method should be applied in approaching them? What language should be used to address them? He deals with the problems of intelligibility and communication brought about by the cultural alienation between the Church and secular society. He also examines postmodern impulses concerning the problem of religious language, such as *deconstruction* (Derrida, Caputo), *hermeneutics* (Kearney), and *phenomenology* (Marion). Finally he turns to Rowan Williams and Tomáš Halík and proposes his own strategy in approaching seekers: he suggests that seekers and dwellers are not polar-opposites but both share the space in the middle between belief and unbelief and argues for a "porous" identity of the Church.

In the sixth chapter entitled "**An Unknown God of Paradox: Tomáš Halík on Faith in a Secular Age**" Martin Kočí and Pavel Roubík deal with Tomáš Halík's approach to religiosity in a postmodern context. They present Halík's understanding of modern secular culture as a non-institutional "heterodox form of Christian faith". In the following part, Halík's philosophical and theological interpretation of the contemporary religious situation (with a special focus on Czech culture) is analyzed and discussed. Part three deals with Halík's reading of the Zacchaeus' story. He reads it as a "parable" of the current (Czech) religious situation. Following Jesus, the Church should reach out to the Zacchaeuses (i.e. seekers) of today. The last part of chapter six deals with Halík's particular theological interpretation of atheism. In an extensive conclusion, the authors formulate critical questions and remarks and suggest possible venues for further elaboration on Halík's original thought.

In the last chapter entitled "**Church for the Seekers**" Tomáš Halík comments on the ways in which the Church and its official representatives have responded and are responding to the contemporary cultural situation. He focuses on the growing and very diverse "grey zone" between traditional believers and convinced atheists, i.e. on the zone of contemporary seekers. He tries to address the following questions: Should the Church function as a comfortable home for dwellers or should it also become an open space for seekers? Should its solidarity with people of our time which the Church promised in the opening sentence of the constitution *Gaudium et spes* imply not only that it will be "crying with those who are crying and rejoicing with those who are rejoicing" but also seeking with those who are seeking?

The essays collected in this volume have been written in friendly interaction and ongoing dialogue among the four authors. Tomáš Halík, the recent Templeton prize winner and the leader of our team, is quite an interesting cultural phenomenon in himself. This is why he is not just one of the authors but also one of the "subjects" of our book. Halík is a professor of sociology at the prestigious Charles University in Prague. At the same time he is a Roman Catholic priest and a papal prelate. Being a faithful representative of the Church, he is at the same time (and paradoxically) one of the most influential public intellectuals in the country. And that, in fact, is quite unique: A loyal son of the Church is well received and highly admired by a society with strong anti-clerical sentiments. His numerous books have been bestsellers for the last fifteen years, he gets invited to national TV and broadcast on a daily basis. It seems quite obvious that many Czech seekers find his humble and kenotic testimony convincing and appealing. No wonder then, that all the remaining members of the team consider him to be their master and guide, especially in the question, which is of major interest for all of them, i.e. how to integrate sociological research and postmodern thought into theological reflection on contemporary culture and how to develop a corresponding missiological approach and methodology, suitable for the Church as it enters into dialogue with contemporary seekers.

The essays presented in this volume form, we hope, a coherent whole: Starting from the historical and sociological analysis of Czech cultural condition, focusing especially on the high degree of secularity and various past and present responses of the Church (the first two chapters), this book offers a more general theological reflection on the origins and nature of European secularity and its complex relation to Christianity (chapters three and four), which is followed by an analysis of several aspects of the postmodern cultural condition and the challenges and opportunities, which that condition presents for the Church (chapters five and six). The final chapter of the volume offers an evaluative commentary on the ways the Church has responded to these challenges and opportunities so far and a reflection on some of the promising and positive ways it may respond in the future.

This future oriented outlook, searching for new and culturally sensitive ways of witnessing to the Gospel is not just the key theme of the final chapter. It is in fact implicitly present throughout the book from the first page to the last, since it is of major concern and lifelong interest for all the four team members who contributed to this volume.

BIBLIOGRAPHY

Fiala, Petr 2007. *The Laboratory of Secularisation: Religion and Politics in a Non-religious Society: the Czech Case (Laboratoř sekularizace. Náboženství a politika v ne-náboženské společnosti: český příklad*) Brno: CDK.
Halík, Tomáš. 2002. *What Does not Shiver is not Firm* (*Co je bez chvění, není pevné*). Praha: Lidové noviny.

Halík, Tomáš. 2004. *Vocatus et Invocatus* (*Vzýván i nevzýván*). Praha: Lidové noviny.
Halík, Tomáš. 2007. *Near to Those who Are Distant* (*Vzdáleným nablízku*). Praha: Lidové noviny.
Halík, Tomáš. 2009. *Hope Remains for the Tree* (*Stromu zbývá naděje*). Praha: Lidové noviny.
Halík, Tomáš. 2010. *Spectacle for the Angels* (*Divadlo pro anděly*). Praha: Lidové noviny.
Halík, Tomáš. 2012. *I Want You to Be* (*Chci, abys byl*). Praha: Lidové noviny.
Hamplová, Dana 2014. *Religion in Czech Society on the Treshhold of the Third Millenium* (*Náboženství v české společnosti na prahu třetího tisíciletí*) Praha: Karolinum.
Taylor, Charles. 2007. *A Secular Age*. Cambridge MT: Harvard University Press.
Tichý, Radek and Vávra, Martin 2012. *Religion from a Different Angle* (*Náboženství z jiného úhlu*). Brno: CDK.

CHAPTER I

DISCERNING THE SIGNS OF THE TIMES IN THE POST-COMMUNIST CZECH REPUBLIC: A HISTORICAL, SOCIOLOGICAL AND MISSIOLOGICAL ANALYSIS OF CONTEMPORARY CZECH CULTURE

PAVEL HOŠEK

Making our own Jesus' recommendation that we learn to discern "the signs of the times", it seems to us that we can make out, in the midst of so much darkness, more than a few indications that enable us to have hope for the fate of the Church and of humanity. (John XXIII, *Humanae Salutis*)

This chapter consists of two parts. The first part provides a historical and sociological survey of Czech religiosity and spirituality. It deals with the developing attitudes and relations of the Czech people towards religion, Church and spiritual values in recent history. The second part builds on the observations and conclusions of the first part. It offers a missiological analysis and commentary on the current cultural situation in the Czech Republic in light of a particular theological hermeneutics of culture, inspired by the guiding metaphor of discerning the signs of the times[1] and a corresponding understanding of the role of Christians in contemporary secular society and culture[2].

RELIGION AND CZECH SOCIETY

Czech society is one of the least religious in the world[3]. According to the most recent census in 2011[4], the three largest

---

[1] Mt 16, 2-3. Cf. John XXIII., *Humanae Salutis*. See also Paul VI., *Evangelii Nuntiandi,* par. 75 and 76, and especially Francis, *Evangelii Gaudium,* par. 51.

[2] Cf. John Paul II., *Centesimus Annus,* par. 50 and 51 and *Christifideles Laici,* par. 44, Benedict XVI., *Caritas in Veritate,* par. 26 and especially Francis, *Evangelii Gaudium,* par. 115, 116, 122 and 257.

[3] Cf. for example O. Nešporová, Z. Nešpor, "Religion: An Unsolved Problem for the Modern Czech Nation,"1 *Czech Sociological Review* 45,

Churches, the Roman Catholic Church, the Evangelical Church of Czech Brethren, and the Czechoslovak Hussite Church, have respectively one million and eighty-three thousand, fifty-two thousand, and thirty-nine thousand adherents, which is indeed remarkably few given that the entire population of the country is a little over ten million people. Some journalists like to repeat the statement that the Czechs are a nation of atheists. But many books and articles have already been written about the inaccuracy of this assertion[5]. There are probably not many more convinced, "professing" atheists in Czech society than in other European countries[6]. Estimates of the number of convinced atheists range between roughly a fifth and a quarter of the population, which more or less corresponds to the proportion of atheists in other societies in Central and Western Europe. The exceptional character of Czech society in relation to religion evidently consists in something other than the number of convinced atheists. The question of why the Czech nation has a very specific and in fact unique relationship to religion is one that has occupied historians, philosophers, sociologists, and theologians for decades.

The Importance of Religion in the Cultural History of the Czech Nation

A number of theories exist about why the Czechs are so indifferent to religion, in particular towards organised religion. Some historians (and especially some Protestant theologians) were for a long time convinced that the origin of the characteristically Czech relationship towards religion and Church was to be found in the traumatic events of the Thirty Years' War (1618-1648), in other words as long ago as the seventeenth century[7]. They saw the origin and root of this very lukewarm, if not negative, attitude of most Czechs towards

---

(2009), 1215-1237, or D. Lužný, J. Navrátilová, "Religion and Secularisation in the Czech Republic," *Czech Sociological Review*, 9 (2001), pp. 85-98.

[4] Cf. the official website of the Czech statistical office www.czso.cz.

[5] Cf. for example D. Hamplová, Z. Nešpor, "Invisible Religion in a Non-believing Country: The Case of the Czech Republic", *Social Compass*, 56 (2009), pp. 581-597. Cf. also R. Tichý, M. Vávra, *Religion from a Different Angle* (*Náboženství z jiného úhlu*) (Brno: CDK, 2012), pp. 11ff.

[6] Z. Nešpor, *Too Weak in Faith. Czech (Non)-religiosity in European Context* (*Příliš slábi ve víře. Česká (ne)religiozita v evropském kontextu*) (Praha: Kalich, 2010), p. 133; D. Václavík, *Religion and Modern Czech Society* (*Náboženství a moderní česká společnost*) (Praha: Grada, 2010), p. 162. See also www.czso.cz

[7] J. Fiala, *Horrible Times of Counter-Reformation* (*Hrozné doby protireformace*), (Heršpice: Eman, 1997), pp. 7ff.

religion in the trauma caused by the forcible re-Catholicisation of the predominantly Protestant nation in the period after the Battle of the White Mountain in 1620. The educated elite of the nation, in other words the non-Catholic nobility, had either to emigrate or else submit to a compulsory and therefore insincere conversion to Catholicism. The rest of the population, the majority of them non-Catholic, had to change their religious affiliation. It is certainly true that the persecution and expulsion of the non-Catholics from the country, together with the policy of re-Catholicisation that was adopted and pursued by the ruling Habsburg dynasty, did cause a profound and long-lasting trauma. Most people at the time were forced to change their religious affiliation, contrary to their own conscience, and spiritual violence of this kind usually has far-reaching historical consequences.

On the other hand, it should be added that the re-Catholicisation appears to have been relatively "successful", and fairly quickly at that[8]. Its proponents soon adopted a far-sighted strategy based on education and work with the younger generation, and in this way were successful in winning over the greater part of the Czech nation to the Catholic faith and religiosity. We have no evidence, for example, that the Catholic faith and religiosity of most of the inhabitants of Bohemia and Moravia in the eighteenth century were in any way lukewarm, inauthentic, or forced, or that people only displayed them outwardly while secretly gritting their teeth and clenching their fists[9].

It seems more likely that the more fundamental causes of the lukewarm attitude of most Czechs towards religion are to be found in a later period, probably during the nineteenth century, in connection with a growing national awareness[10]. In the search for the emerging identity of the Czech nation and of greater cultural and national self-confidence, a factor that logically presented itself was a negative delimitation against the pressure of Germanisation on the part of the German-speaking Habsburg monarchs. The period before the accession of the Habsburgs to the throne of Bohemia – in other words the era of Charles IV, the period from the time of Jan Hus to King George of Poděbrady, and later

---

[8] D. Václavík, *Religion and Modern Czech Society*, pp. 53ff.
[9] D. Václavík, *Religion and Modern Czech Society*, p. 57.
[10] Z. Nešpor, *Too Weak in Faith. Czech (Non)-religiosity in European Context*, 10, 50ff; D. Hamplová, *Religion in Czech Society on the Treshhold of the Third Millenium (Náboženství v české společnosti na prahu třetího tisíciletí)* (Praha: Karolinum, 2013), p. 23; P. Fiala, *The Laboratory of Secularisation: Religion and Politics in a Non-religious Society: the Czech Case (Laboratoř sekularizace. Náboženství a politika v ne-náboženské společnosti: český příklad)* (Brno: CDK, 2007), p. 28.

(already under Habsburg rule), the age of the flowering of Czech Protestant culture before the Battle of the White Mountain – was seen by the Czech patriots and architects of the national revival as the "golden age of Czech history" and the "supreme era of Czech culture", which was followed by a lamentable decline and a long period of stagnation[11]. The period that was symbolically bookended by the figures of Jan Hus (1370 – 1415) and Jan Amos Comenius (1592 – 1670) appeared in the nineteenth century to be the most suitable building material for shaping the Czech national identity and the source of the symbols of Czech national pride[12].

For many of the architects of the Czech national revival, therefore, a shadow of ill will also fell on the religious affiliation of those who put an end to this "supreme period of Czech history". The Habsburgs were unable to shake off the suspicion that with their pressure to Germanise and re-Catholicise they were "enemies of the distinctive national and cultural character of the Czech nation". The Habsburg monarchs began to be portrayed as more or less unwelcome foreigners who were forcing something on the Czech nation that was in some way alien to them. This also explained the profound cultural decline in the Czech lands after the Thirty Years' War.

The generation that saw the rise of the Czech national revival thus interpreted the key events and processes of Czech history up to that point in a certain way, and arrived at a specific interpretation or "retelling" of its "most important themes". Later this interpretation was reinforced by the psychological explanation of allegedly typical characteristics of the Czech national character, such as being a clever fool like the Good Soldier Švejk, readiness to accommodate to fit in with the circumstances, craftiness, and other unattractive qualities of "small-minded, cynical people with warped characters". These features were supposed to have been caused by centuries of political and cultural mutilation of the Czech nation through the Habsburg policies of Germanisation and re-Catholicisation[13]. Regardless of how much truth

---

[11] J. Fiala, *Horrible Times of Counter-Reformation*, pp. 75ff; Z. Nešpor, *Too Weak in Faith. Czech (Non)-religiosity in European Context*, pp. 8-9; J. Malíř, "Secularisation and Politics in the 'Long' Nineteenth Century," in L. Fasora, J. Hanuš, J. Malíř (eds.), *Secularisation of Czech Lands between 1848 and 1914 (Sekularizace v českých zemích v letech 1848-1914)* (Brno: CDK, 2007), p. 19.

[12] Z. Nešpor, "The so called Czech Atheism and Its Social and Ecclesial Consequences," in *Czech Atheism. Causes, Positives, Negatives (Český ateismus. Příčiny, klady, zápory)* (Benešov: Eman, 2006), p. 75.

[13] D. Václavík, *Religion and Modern Czech Society*, pp. 72-73.

these popular interpretations contained, their dissemination understandably led to a distinct coolness on the part of a significant section of Czech society in relation to the majority religion that was granted a privileged position by the Habsburg dynasty.

All of this was reinforced by a series of modernising trends in the nineteenth century such as liberalisation, urbanisation, industrialisation (the Czech lands were the "industrial heart of the Austro-Hungarian state"), and also the gradual establishment of a social class of influential intellectuals and political commentators, who frequently held liberal views and rather critical attitudes towards religious institutions[14]. These social trends further deepened the alienation felt by a large part of Czech society in relation to the official religion. However, this did not mean that large numbers of people left the Church or converted to non-Catholic Churches, whose existence had been legalised by the Edict of Tolerance issued by Joseph II in 1781. Virtually all the proponents of this "anticlerical interpretation" of Czech history and culture remained members of the Roman Catholic Church until their dying day. It was more a case of a gradual inner coolness and indifference in their relationship to the Church developing, and step by step even among the members of the Roman Catholic Church the typical Czech suspicion established itself that the Church was primarily concerned with power and money, and that it was less interested in the welfare of the Czech nation than in its own profit and the favour of the powerful.

Distrust of the Church

According to a number of surveys, the Czechs do not differ from other nations so much in the number of atheists as in the degree of distrust of religious institutions[15]. This distrust of the Churches is so high in the Czech nation that it appears to outstrip the degree of distrust of the Churches in countries that probably have even a slightly higher percentage of atheists (such as the former East Germany or Estonia).

---

[14] Z. Nešpor, *Too Weak in Faith. Czech (Non)-religiosity in European Context*, pp. 40-41. Cf. P. Berger, G. Davie, E. Fokas, *Religious America, Secular Europe?* (Burlington: Ashgate, 2008), pp. 54ff.

[15] M. Quesnell, *What Do We Think, What Do We Believe In and Who We Are* (*Co si myslíme, čemu věříme a kdo jsme*) (Praha: Academia, 2002), pp. 65ff, D. Václavík, *Religion and Modern Czech Society*, p. 162; D. Hamplová, *Religion in Czech Society on the Treshhold of the Third Millenium*, pp. 8 and 49ff; J. Spousta, "Czech Churches through the Eyes of Sociological Research," in J. Hanuš (ed.), *Religion in the Time of Social Changes* (*Náboženství v době společenských změn*) (Brno: Masarykova Univerzita, 1999), p. 82.

This high percentage of Czechs who distrust the Church indicates that this distrust is harboured not only by non-Church people looking at the Church from outside, but also by a significant percentage of those who are themselves Church members.

To some extent, of course, this is connected with the lapses and sins of the representatives of the Church which come to light from time to time and arouse public outrage. But all the indications are that the Church in the Czech lands is neither more sinful nor more avaricious than it is in other countries where people trust it much more. Indeed, it is quite possible that the Czech Church is in a better condition than is the case in countries where the majority of the population profess to be members, and where there is consequently far more opportunity for corruption and "degeneracy" among laypeople and its leading representatives. At all events, the Czech Church has to withstand the close attention of journalists and the more or less suspicious gaze of a large part of the Czech public, which has a certain cultivating effect on it, as it cannot count on any indulgence or forbearing benevolence on the part of the media and the majority of society.

It would seem that this suspicious attitude of Czech society towards the Church, which is still evident today, has its origin in that specific interpretation of Czech history which became part of the national and cultural self-understanding of many generations of Czechs. This self-understanding probably then gradually began to have the magical effect of a self-fulfilling prophecy. Political commentators, literary figures, and others who helped shape public opinion interpreted, and sometimes today still interpret, Czech history from an "anti-clerical" perspective, and because they have had a substantial influence in Czech society and have to a considerable extent helped fashion public awareness, this half-truth, when it was repeated a hundred times, became a reality, in other words a catalyst for a genuine indifference, a genuine inner (though not necessarily external) split between the greater part of Czech society and the Church[16].

Religion in Free Czechoslovakia

After the break-up of the Austro-Hungarian state in 1918, the

---

[16] It is obvious why due to this situation, the so called "vicarious religion" does not seem to be a common phenomenon in Czech society, see Z. Nešpor, *Too Weak in Faith. Czech (Non)-religiosity in European Context*, p. 136. Similarly, "belonging without believing" (cf. P. Berger, G. Davie, E. Fokas, *Religious America, Secular Europe?*, p. 39) does not seem to be very common in Czech culture.

architects of the idea of a free Czechoslovakia interpreted the "meaning of Czech history" and its most important themes in the spirit indicated above. It was by no means an anti-Christian interpretation. It included, for example, highlighting and at times to a certain extent idealising the Unity of Brethren. But it was an interpretation that was in an important sense of the word anti-clerical[17]. The whole of the period before the Battle of the White Mountain was seen as the golden age of Czech culture, which was followed by decline and decay, and a return to the legacy of that period was needed. During the First Czechoslovak Republic (in the interwar years) non-Catholic forms of faith, religiosity, and Church structure enjoyed considerable favour from the highest representatives of the state (including the first president and number one hero of free Czechoslovakia T. G. Masaryk)[18]. As part of what was known as the "conversion movement", a new Church was founded, the Czechoslovak Hussite Church, and within a short space of time several hundred thousand people had joined it (nearly all former Roman Catholics). However, these conversions often took place more for patriotic or cultural reasons than religious ones. For many Czechs it was a symbolic confirmation of the "break with Vienna" (the seat of the Habsburg monarchy), which now culminated in a "break with Rome" as well.

The "conversion movement" also led to an increase in the number of Protestants. The two large Churches that came into being after the First World War and considered themselves to be the heirs of the Czech Reformation – the new Czechoslovak Hussite Church and the Evangelical Church of Czech Brethren that was created through the union of Czech Calvinists and Lutherans – could not compete with the majority Roman Catholic Church in terms of numbers, but during the period of the First Republic they were supported as being the upholders of the best traditions of the Czech nation.

In the interwar period, during the Second World War, and immediately after it, the alienation between the Church and a large part of the Czech public increased due to a shift of many Czech intellectuals towards the left. Some of them became enthusiastic communists, while others tended towards a more moderate form of left-wing philosophy. The socialist workers' movement, of which they became spokespeople, was generally suspicious of and hostile towards the Church. The working class, which came into being as a new and very numerous social class during the course of the industrial revolution in the

---

[17] P. Fiala, *The Laboratory of Secularisation: Religion and Politics in a Non-religious Society: the Czech Case*, p. 35.

[18] D. Václavík, *Religion and Modern Czech Society*, pp. 53, 61 and 68.

nineteenth century, generally felt that it had been betrayed by the Church. Not without some justification, the working class accused the Church of not taking much interest in their unfavourable conditions, because it preferred to make friends with the "rich factory-owners", in other words with their "exploiters". Nor was the Church quick enough in initiating pastoral care for the working class, so it seemed that it was simply abandoning the workers to their poverty. The emancipatory working-class movement therefore often adopted a mistrustful and hostile attitude towards the Church, and itself fulfilled the role of a "substitute religion" for its adherents[19].

However, the increasing coolness in the relationship to the Church during the course of the first half of the twentieth century mostly did not lead to people officially leaving it. Even the first census carried out after the communist takeover of power represented an unpleasant surprise for the architects of a policy of "atheisation". In this census, taken in 1950, more than ninety per cent of the population said they had some sort of Church affiliation[20].

Another factor influencing the gradual decline in the significance of the public role of the Church in postwar Czechoslovakia was the expulsion of the Sudeten Germans from the country under the terms of the Beneš decrees. The majority of the Germans who left the country were members of the Roman Catholic Church[21]. The people who were moved into the empty Sudeten lands to take their place came mostly from the lower social classes, and had a strong left-wing orientation and a lukewarm (or negative) relationship to the Church.

Religion in the Communist Period

During the period of the communist regime[22], which came to power in February 1948, the Church was subjected to various forms of persecution and repression. In the 1950s, the anti-Church policy

---

[19] Z. Nešpor, *Too Weak in Faith. Czech (Non)-religiosity in European Context*, pp. 42ff.

[20] D. Václavík, *Religion and Modern Czech Society*, pp. 105-106.

[21] D. Václavík, *Religion and Modern Czech Society*, pp. 96-97.

[22] Cf. especially V. Vaško, *She Was not Silenced. Chronicle of the Catholic Church in Czechoslovakia after the Second World War* (*Neumlčená. Kronika katolické církve v Československu po druhé světové válce*), vol. I. and II., (Praha: Zvon, 1990). See also D. Václavík, *Religion and Modern Czech Society*, pp. 93ff; Z. Nešpor, *Too Weak in Faith. Czech (Non)-religiosity in European Context*, pp. 60ff; D. Hamplová, *Religion in Czech Society on the Treshhold of the Third Millenium*, p. 25.

followed the model of the Soviet Union in using fairly primitive methods of persecution. In the 1960s this was followed by a gradual improvement in relations between the state and the Church, and for a certain period it seemed as though a new and friendlier way of coexistence between the ruling regime and the Czech Church would be created. However, this hope associated with the end of the 1960s was ended by the invasion of the Warsaw Pact troops on 21 August 1968. Immediately after this the period known as "normalisation" started, which was devastating for the Czech Church[23]. This was not because any harsh or vigorous repression occurred. In comparison with the repression of the 1950s the approach adopted by the state was more moderate. However, the communist regime opted for the tactic of "pushing the Church into the Church buildings". The Church gradually became an isolated sub-culture without any opportunity to act in the public domain[24]. The members of the Church grew used to this arrangement, and at times they even began to feel that it suited them. The communist government then adopted the tactic of calmly waiting for the Churches to die quietly. It continued with the bureaucratic harassment of the priests and ministers and surveillance by the state officials known as Church secretaries and with the infiltration of the Church by agents and informers of the secret police, and in this way attempted to assist the slow but certain weakening and disappearance of the Church.

The gradual "demoralisation of the nation" and the weakening of the Church was also encouraged by the shift in priorities of a large part of Czech society (inconspicuously orchestrated by the communist government) towards a specific type of consumerism. The ruling regime opted for the tactic of promoting a somewhat materially oriented lifestyle focused on constantly trying to find and buy cars, televisions, washing machines, refrigerators, weekend cottages, and holidays in Yugoslavia, leading to the notorious "goulash socialism" of the normalisation years[25].

According to surveys carried out in the normalisation period, however, most Czechs did not agree with the compulsory "atheisation" of society. People did not want a repressive approach to the Church and its representatives. A large number of respondents were even in favour of broadcasting Church services on the radio, in other words precisely the form of Church proclamation where listening to it could not be

---

[23] D. Václavík, *Religion and Modern Czech Society*, pp. 115ff.
[24] Z. Nešpor, *Too Weak in Faith. Czech (Non)-religiosity in European Context*, p. 76.
[25] D. Václavík, *Religion and Modern Czech Society*, p. 120.

monitored from the outside, and which therefore could not be under the surveillance of the state machinery.

From the observations we have made so far it would seem that the forty years of the communist regime does not appear to have brought about any fundamental atheisation of society in itself. This was because the Czechs were already fairly indifferent to religion in 1948, in spite of the fact that the vast majority of them were still Church members. However, their relationship to faith and to the Church was a loose one, and in large part formal and the result of force of habit. What the communists achieved was to bring about the gradual disappearance of this faith based on force of habit and lacking in depth. A change of generation had taken place. The generation born after 1948 marks a turning-point in this regard. For this is precisely the generation that ceased to identify with the Church and stopped going to Church. It seemed that a turning-point had occurred[26]: the people born in the 1950s, whose parents had still nearly all belonged to the Church, in the vast majority of cases ceased to be Church-goers, either not going to Church at all, or else only very rarely. However, this "turning-point" would not have occurred if the faith of the parents of these "children of socialism" had not been to a considerable extent a matter of force of habit and lukewarm. It is worth noting that in other countries in the Soviet bloc such a far-reaching change did not occur. The striking difference between the Czech and Slovak parts of Czechoslovakia also speaks for itself in this regard. In the case of the Czech Republic all that the communist regime actually did was simply to give a helping hand to the gradual extinction of the formal, shallow faith of the 1950s.

For a large part of the population, however, the persecution of Christians during the period of communist totality tended to arouse sympathy for the Church. Many Catholic priests were imprisoned and harassed in all sorts of ways by the communist regime. Much of the population in the countries under Soviet domination greatly appreciated the Pope's uncompromising stance towards the communist ideology and his influence on the political events that culminated in the break-up of the Soviet bloc and the collapse of the communist regimes there. This meant that after the "Velvet Revolution" of 1989 the Church was viewed in quite a positive light by a substantial proportion of the Czech public[27]. According to a survey in 1990, 51% of the population had confidence in

---

[26] Z. Nešpor, *Too Weak in Faith. Czech (Non)-religiosity in European Context*, pp. 81 and 87.

[27] Z. Nešpor, *Too Weak in Faith. Czech (Non)-religiosity in European Context*, p. 98; P. Fiala, *The Laboratory of Secularisation: Religion and Politics in a Non-religious Society: the Czech Case*, p. 38.

the Churches. In the census carried out in 1991[28], 44% of the population professed some form of religious affiliation, with no less than 39% saying they were Roman Catholics. 203,000 people said they were adherents of the Evangelical Church of Czech Brethren, and 178,000 professed adherence to the Czechoslovak Hussite Church.

Religion after the Velvet Revolution

However, this wave of popularity for the Church faded quite quickly. The hopes that had been placed in the Church were not fulfilled, and very soon the traditional distrust of religious institutions made its presence felt again – something in which the Czechs really excel. To give an accurate picture, however, we should add that this distrust does not just relate to religious institutions. The Czechs have a deeply-rooted and fundamental distrust of institutions in general[29]. A typical assumption of a large part of Czech society is the suspicion that institutions do not pursue the interests of the citizens they are supposed to serve, but in reality just serve themselves and only pursue their own interests in the form of power and money. The Czech distrust of religious institutions is a specific example of this general phenomenon.

Even in the period when the majority of Czechs had confidence in the Church, they clearly did not want a rich and powerful one. The wanted a Church that was noble-minded, humble, and ready to serve, a Church that was modest and self-sacrificing. But they did not, and still do not, want a Church that is rich and powerful[30]. That is why they are very allergic in their reaction, whenever it appears that the Church aspires to political power or engages in a struggle with politicians over property. The reputation and credibility of the Czech Church have always been severely damaged by disputes over the restitution of Church property, "nationalized" (i.e. stolen) by the communist government. Unfortunately, when the Church vehemently demands the return of its property that was stolen by the communists, in the minds of many

---

[28] Cf. www.czso.cz

[29] Cf. M. Sedláčková, Trust and Democracy in the Czech Society, in Z. Jurechová Z., P. Bargár (eds.), *Crisis Situations in the Czecho-Slovak Context after 1989* (Praha: CECMS, 2011), pp. 60ff.

[30] P. Fiala, *The Laboratory of Secularisation: Religion and Politics in a Non-religious Society: the Czech Case*, pp. 61ff; Z. Nešpor, *Too Weak in Faith. Czech (Non)-religiosity in European Context*, p. 99, see also J. Spousta, Czech Churches through the Eyes of Sociological Research, in J. Hanuš (ed.), *Religion in the Time of Social Changes*, p. 88.

people they correspond precisely to the centuries-old stereotype of "covetous prelates".

The 1991 census was followed ten years later by another one, in which the three largest Churches all recorded a substantial drop in the number of their adherents. In 2001[31], 2,740,000 inhabitants of the Czech Republic declared that they were members of the Roman Catholic Church, 117,000 said they were adherents of the Evangelical Church of Czech Brethren, and 99,000 professed adherence to the Czechoslovak Hussite Church, while the largest Churches recorded a considerable decline in membership, the numbers of adherents of the small Protestant Churches increased. However, it should be emphasised that the members of these smaller denominations are numbered in the thousands.

Both these trends, the decrease in membership of all three large Churches and the gradual increase in the number of adherents of the small Protestant Churches, is still continuing, as can be seen from the results of the most recent census in 2011. While slightly more than 1,083,000 citizens of the Czech Republic declared themselves to be members of the Roman Catholic Church and the corresponding numbers for the Evangelical Church of Czech Brethren and the Czechoslovak Hussite Church were 52,000 and 39,000 respectively, the number of adherents of the smaller Protestant Churches (the Church of Brethren, the Christian Communities Church, the Apostolic Church, the Czech Baptist Union, the Christian Congregations, the Moravian Church, the Evangelical Methodist Church, and other denominations) either remained the same, in some cases dropped slightly, or in many cases increased considerably.

On the other hand it should be noted that according to the internal statistics of the Churches and according to specialised surveys the number of practising believers and of those regularly attending Church services has not declined dramatically over the last ten years. The drop in membership thus concerns primarily those who are members "on paper" only and non-practising Christians. Another important factor is of course the age range of Church members and the considerable difference in the proportion of the younger generations between the individual Churches.

At the same time it is quite obvious that the general trend away from traditional Church religiosity, which can be observed in virtually all countries of the Western culture, is also characteristic for the Czech

---

[31] Cf. www.czso.cz. See also I. Štampach, "Religious Spectrum of the Czech Republic," in J. Hanuš (ed.), *Religion in the Time of Social Changes*, pp. 65ff and J. Spousta, "Czech Churches through the Eyes of Sociological Research," in J. Hanuš (ed.), *Religion in the Time of Social Changes*, pp. 73ff.

situation, and indeed is reinforced here by some typical attitudes of Czech society towards religion, which, as we have seen, have deep historical roots.

In the light of the results of the most recent census it is also quite clear that Christians in the Czech Republic are a non-conformist minority. This of course brings with it a number of disadvantages. On the other hand, their minority status seems to be a cultivating factor: the Czech Churches are not in the position of privileged institutions pampered by the powers that be, as is often the case in countries where it pays the state to shower the majority Church with all sorts of privileges so as to ensure it influences the views of voters. In the Czech situation Church membership does not imply any advantages, which evidently results in a certain (at least relative) purity of motivation of those who profess to be believers and Church members[32].

The typical Czech mistrust of religious institutions is reflected in the results of the censuses in the fact that new religious movements of a "sectarian type" appear to have already reached the zenith of their growth in the Czech lands some years ago and now are declining. The period in which they flourished the most was in the mid-1990s, and one of the main reasons was the spiritual vacuum created by the communist regime, which banned the missionary activity of these movements. As can be seen from the decline in the number of adherents of the new religious movements of a sectarian type over the past fifteen years, religious groups which make high demands on the private life, financial generosity and lifestyle of their members evidently cannot achieve much success in a society with a profound mistrust of religious organisations. Czech society simply has a very grudging, if not downright hostile, attitude to cults and groups of sectarian nature[33].

The gradual decline in the influence of religious institutions (and of their normative interpretations of tradition) on the personal and spiritual life of individuals is also evident in the remarkable lack of orthodoxy among Czech believers. Surveys show that Czech Christians are exceptionally non-orthodox. The number of Czech Christians who believe in reincarnation, or who do not believe in the divinity of Jesus Christ, the doctrine of the Trinity, and other defining elements of Church

---

[32] P. Fiala, *The Laboratory of Secularisation: Religion and Politics in a Non-religious Society: the Czech Case*, p. 155; J. Spousta, "Czech Churches through the Eyes of Sociological Research," in J. Hanuš (ed.), *Religion in the Time of Social Changes*, p. 81.

[33] Z. Vojtíšek, *New Religious Movements and How to Understand Them* (*Nová náboženská hnutí a jak jim porozumět*) (Praha: Beta Books, 2007), pp. 25ff and 193ff.

orthodoxy, is very high[34]. This applies understandably primarily to the three largest Czech Churches; in the small Protestant denominations, on the contrary, the overall degree of "orthodoxy" (or doctrinal conformity) is traditionally high.

In this respect, too, Czech society follows the general trend of a move away from Church religiosity and the weakening of the influence of normative interpretations of tradition. And here again this general trend seems to be more far-reaching in the Czech setting than in some other countries, and probably this is once again the result of the fundamental mistrust of a large part of Czech society towards the Church, which we have already referred to a number of times. Even those Czechs who are Christians do not often let the Church dictate to them how and what they will believe. In addition, since even those Czechs who are Christians do not go to Church all that often and do not take part in regular Church activities, which are the instruments for character formation and for passing on Church teaching, the Church does not in fact have too many opportunities to influence their lives and form their opinions by means of its normative interpretations.

It is interesting to note that Czech atheists do not seem to be particularly orthodox in their atheism, either. According to a number of surveys, those citizens of the Czech Republic who either profess themselves to be atheists or say that they are without religious affiliation (which does not have to be the same thing), admit the existence of supernatural phenomena and take an interest in them. Between a third and a half of Czechs admit the possibility of foretelling the future by means of horoscopes. Between a third and a half of Czechs are open to the effectiveness of magic amulets. Many Czechs are also inclined to believe in the supranatural abilities to foresee future events and heal diseases[35]. A substantial proportion of those who did not answer the question about religious faith in the census (it was optional), and probably even of those who answered that they do not have any religious faith, evidently cannot be regarded as proper "materialistic atheists". In addition to those who are completely indifferent to questions related to religion, these groups evidently contain a high percentage of "something-ists", in other words adherents of the more or less clearly articulated conviction that there most probably is "something" above us, but that it is not advisable or necessary to give it a concrete outline, and

---

[34] Z. Nešpor, *Too Weak in Faith. Czech (Non)-religiosity in European Context*, p. 132.

[35] D. Hamplová, *Religion in Czech Society on the Treshhold of the Third Millenium*, pp. 59ff.

definitely not a form that would be in some way obligatory or observable from the outside.

"Something-ism", defined in this way, corresponds quite well to the "Jedi religion", inspired by the *Star Wars* film saga. Adherents of Jediism profess simple ethical principles and venerate the universal mystical Force. During the last census, "out of nowhere" no less than 15,000 people declared their affiliation to this "religion"[36]. Quite a few of them no doubt intended this as a joke or intended it (like some "adherents" of Jediism in other countries) simply as a way of boycotting the attempt by the state to monitor the religious orientation of the population. However, a certain similarity between typical Czech "something-ism" and the religious philosophy of Jediism is certainly worth examining. Czech "something-ism" is incidentally also quite easily compatible with the loosely defined New Age movement, to which up to a million people in the Czech Republic probably adhere to some extent.

From the prosperity of bookshops with spiritually oriented literature it is clear that a substantial proportion of the Czech public takes an intensive interest in non-materialistic interpretations of reality, admittedly often in relation to an alternative lifestyle, a healthy diet, physical exercise, ecology, life in harmony with natural or cosmic energy, and so on. It is therefore not surprising that according to the 2011 census there are almost three-quarters of a million people in the Czech Republic who consider themselves to be believers but at the same time refuse to identify themselves with any particular religious tradition and Church. They form the second largest religious "group" in the country (after the Roman Catholic Church).

It is also interesting that nearly half the population of the Czech Republic (4,770,000 people) refused to answer the question about religious belief. This is probably testimony to the typical Czech mistrust of institutions (and their prying into the private lives of citizens), and also to the fact that the religious landscape of Czech society can be an unusually rugged one. For these people for some reason chose not to tick the box "without religious belief" (which was ticked by 3,600,000 people).

One of the reasons why so many people did not answer this question about religion and why there is a relatively large number of people in our country who are believers in some sense, but who refuse to give a concrete content to their belief and refuse to identify it with the categories offered, is perhaps the proverbial "shyness" of the faith of the

---

[36] Cf. www.czso.cz.

Czech nation. In view of their historical experiences described above, Czechs are remarkably "timid" and "bashful" when it comes to their belief and the ways they manifest it – so bashful that they usually consider their belief or religiosity to be too intimate a subject for them to declare and display it publically[37].

MISSIOLOGICAL CONSIDERATIONS

In the following section of this chapter I would like to offer a missiological reflection on the above described contemporary condition of Czech culture and society in relation to religion, Church, faith and spirituality. As I indicated in the beginning, this reflection is guided by the metaphor of discerning the signs of the times and seeking an adequate Christian response to contemporary cultural situation.

Contemporary Czech Culture as a Marketplace

The current cultural situation in the post-communist Czech Republic can be quite aptly illustrated (especially in comparision with the previous historical period) by the metaphor of a marketplace. There are two important reasons for this. Firstly, a characteristic sign of contemporary Czech culture (in contrast with the communist period) is colourful and varied plurality and abundance. Secondly, almost everything that competes for people's attention in the post-communist cultural situation (including such areas as health and social care, education, politics and religion) is presented as attractive wares offered to be tasted, tried, and bought.

First let us consider the factor of abundance: contemporary Czech culture (in sharp contrast with the communist grey monotony) is characterised by a colourful mosaic of possibilities, promises, and offers, which bombard people's consciousness twenty-four hours a day. For many Czechs, it is becoming difficult to find one's orientation in this flood of words and surfeit of information. The consciousness of many people is fragmented and overburdened, and furthermore they have to wage a frustrating struggle with helplessness, because they are constantly forced to choose and select, but they have no criteria to help them decide which offers and promises can be believed and which cannot.

---

[37] Cf. P. Fiala, *The Laboratory of Secularisation: Religion and Politics in a Non-religious Society: the Czech Case*, pp. 36-37.

Not only are people swamped by data and offers, but often they have no means of organising the individual pieces of information in mutually unrelated areas into meaningful connections. The field of consciousness is getting "fragmented", because it is exposed to sets of information that have no obvious connection, and nobody knows where to find out about such a connection, if it happens to exist.

This typical feature of contemporary Czech culture has some disquieting psychological consequences. In earlier generations and also during the communist times the identity of individuals was relatively firmly rooted in their membership in their family, local community, political party etc., but today all these traditional forms in which identities used to be rooted are very much weakened and no longer provide most people with a point of focus for their identity. A growing number of people now lack this orienting focus and root for their own identity[38].

A second important characteristic of contemporary Czech culture which makes the metaphor of the marketplace appropriate is the fact that the law of supply and demand is becoming more and more important as an all-encompassing framework of social interaction. Just as in every marketplace everything you see can be bought, so almost everything which is offered to the attention of contemporary Czech people is offered to them as "goods" intended for hedonistic consumption[39].

The dynamics of buying and selling, advertising, and the competition for customers, is becoming a key to interpreting an ever broader range of aspects of society, including dimensions that previously had little in common with this, from politics, the health service, and education, through science, to culture and religion. This situation is of course in sharp contrast with the communist past. In an increasingly broader range of social interaction, contemporary Czechs play the role of customers.

The Return of the Sacred

If we develop the metaphorical depiction of contemporary Czech culture as a marketplace a bit further, we can say that in recent decades "traders in the sacred" have made their appearance among the stalls in this marketplace. It would seem that "the sacred" is one of those "goods" for which demand is increasing[40]. More and more often in the Czech

---

[38] Cf. L. Prudký, *Then and Now. Czech Society after 20 years*, pp. 108ff.
[39] L. Prudký, *Then and Now. Czech Society after 20 years* (Plzeň: Vyd. Aleš Čeněk, 2010), pp. 105 and 110.
[40] Cf. D. Václavík, *Religion and Modern Czech Society*, p. 158.

cultural marketplace we find sales points with a more or less serious range of spiritual goods, including ritual aids, meditation courses, spiritual literature, and so on. We can find here a large number of different providers of spiritual and religious values, experiences, and objects, and it seems that goods of this kind sell very well[41].

Although the influence of established traditions and religious institutions on the private life and lifestyle of individuals continues to weaken, as we have seen above, statistics show at the same time an obvious growth in religiosity and spirituality and a "decline of atheism". This renewed interest in spiritual values most often takes the form of privatised syncretism[42]. The consumers of spiritual "goods" take on the role of customers who order and purchase religious products from various suppliers on the basis of clever marketing and well thought-out public relations, simply according to the principles of the free market.

For example, the consumption of horoscopes and amulets in the Czech Republic is surprisingly high and in no way lags behind the consumption of similar goods in countries with a much higher religiosity[43]. Experimenting in the field of the supernatural, the spiritual, or the sacred, whether for amusement or with a more seriously motivation, is evidently becoming a welcome life-enhancing feature, the object of consumption and enjoyment, and a promising commercial article.

Naturally, in this way a new form of religious faith and a new kind of attitude towards spiritual values are gradually developing. For the very reason that spirituality is becoming an interesting field for experimenting in and an item of consumption and enjoyment, a phenomenon is appearing that we can call "do-it-yourself religion", in other words the creation of one's own "spiritual menu", tailor-made for the needs of the specific "handyman", the individual consumer.

Many people develop an experimental and uncommitted approach to spirituality. If they decide to use established spiritual traditions and/or Christian values as parts of their spiritual journey, they adopt a playful and inventive approach towards them.

---

[41] D. Václavík, *Religion and Modern Czech Society*, pp. 168, 196f, see also Z. Nešpor, *Too Weak in Faith. Czech (Non)-religiosity in European Context*, pp. 121-122; Z. Nešpor, The so called Czech Atheism and Its Social and Ecclesial Consequences, in *Czech Atheism. Causes, Positives, Negatives*, pp. 77-78.

[42] D. Václavík, *Religion and Modern Czech Society*, pp. 159ff.

[43] Z. Nešpor, *Too Weak in Faith. Czech (Non)-religiosity in European Context*, p. 127; D. Hamplová, *Religion in Czech Society on the Treshhold of the Third Millenium*, p. 8, 15 and 58ff.

In view of the fact that the Church can offer from the richness of its thousand-year history many different inspiring symbols, values and other elements for contemporary seekers, its importance as a source of inspiration will probably not decline. But it goes without saying that a fundamental transformation of religious motivation is taking place, aptly described as a shift "from obligation to consumption"[44], and "from organised religion to personal spirituality" or "from responsible membership in institutions to a free association of friends".

Official membership in religious institutions, committing members to observe prescribed rules and attitudes to life, is understandably not very popular in contemporary Czech society and culture as we have seen. This is why most religious congregations are losing members and the traditional established religious institutions are showing a loss in the number of active adherents. People who have been baptised in the Church usually do not leave it openly, but hardly ever participate in its organised activities. Among these people, a lukewarm yet benevolent attitude still prevails towards the Church, although sometimes the condition for this benevolence is that the Church does not interfere in the private lives of individuals.

Discerning the Signs of the Times

As implied in the above mentioned theological hermeneutics of culture, guided by the metaphor of discerning the signs of the times, the calling of the Czech Church includes listening attentively to, and trying to understand, the questions that Czech people are asking today, and that they articulate in one way or another in contemporary cultural forms and expressions. As is clearly articulated in the conciliar document *Gaudium et Spes*, Christians of all times and places cannot do other than take the culture of their non-Christian contemporaries with utmost seriousness. For Czech Christians today, this implies being well versed in contemporary Czech culture, and searching for ways to engage it in a meaningful dialogue.

Reading the signs of the times in contemporary Czech cultural context, in other words, searching for points at which to engage in a meaningful dialogue with contemporary seekers seems to be the most appropriate (perhaps the only possible) missiological perspective in the predominantly secular Czech cultural context. In the concluding part of this chapter I am suggesting several promising areas of meaningful

---

[44] Cf. P. Berger, G. Davie, E. Fokas, *Religious America, Secular Europe?*, p. 39.

dialogue (between Czech Christians and contemporary seekers) related to several observable features and obvious general characteristics of the contemporary Czech cultural situation.

The Post-Rationalist Period

In many respects, contemporary Czech culture (just like many other cultures today[45]) is becoming a *post-rationalist* culture, as is apparent especially among young people[46]. The glory of Enlightenment scientific rationalism, as promoted, preached, misused and discredited by the communist government, has to a large extent declined. Although science and its applications in technology still enjoy general popularity and esteem, in contemporary Europe, which has learnt bitter lessons from the failure and abuse of Enlightenment rationality in the two World Wars and the two totalitarian regimes of the twentieth century (both of which affected the Czech Republic drastically), very few people optimistically expect a happy future for the human race to come from scientific and technological progress.

In addition, the younger generation of Czechs, in particular, has come to the realisation that "reason is not everything", that a scientific view of the world does not exhaust all the levels and dimensions of reality, and that other, non-rational approaches to reality may probably become "authentic sources of knowledge". This does not mean that they have to compete with rational knowledge; on the contrary, they can complement and extend it. In short, contemporary young people are rediscovering and appreciating the non-rational components of the human spirit: imagination, intuition, emotion, and spiritual experience. This is characterised by the high value it sets on authentic experience.

Moreover, contemporary youth culture is "rediscovering" the body, the fact that human beings are not simply reason enclosed in a body as if in a diving-suit. All that is physical, sensory, and perceptive is a quintessential part of the human being. The body is becoming an instrument of creative self-expression, a possibility for self-realisation, a work of art, and in addition an appreciative receptor of aesthetic experiences. The contemporary "discovery of the body" is also connected with the search for non-rational forms of perception, the development of fantasy and intuition, and also a new perceptiveness in

---

[45] Cf. D. Bosch, *Transforming Mission. Paradigm Shifts in Theology of Mission* (New York: Orbis Books, 1991), pp. 349ff.

[46] Cf. for example M. Quesnell, *What Do We Think, What Do We Believe In and Who We Are*, pp. 170ff.

relation to the unity between human beings and nature, and a new sensitivity to the environment[47].

All these contemporary cultural "discoveries" can be viewed by Christians with suspicion and mistrust. Fortunately, the attitude of grim mistrust of the values and "discoveries" of contemporary culture is not the only option. In the way the human being is viewed in the Bible we can genuinely find many motifs and values that contemporary culture is today "discovering" again. In this matter contemporary culture is not polemicizing against Christianity, but against modernity, in other words against Enlightenment rationalism and its idolatry of reason and fear of "irrationality", or against the Cartesian notion of the human being as a "ghost in a machine"[48]. But Christianity never agreed with the rationalist reduction of the human being, or, where it did agree, it should not have done. So the way the human being is viewed in the Bible rejects any reduction to rationality. In this sense, the post-rationalist tendency of contemporary Czech culture opens an interesting opportunity for dialogue with contemporary seekers.

The Post-Ideological Period

Contemporary Czech culture is also a *post-ideological* culture. The great ideologies of the Enlightenment have lost their persuasive power and their motivating potential in Czech society, especially due to the painful experience with the oppressive communist state ideology. Furthermore, the contemporary confusing plurality of ideologies on offer has reduced the credibility of each of them. The flood of proofs and arguments in favour of a wide range of ideological interpretations of the world has led to a gradual devaluation of each of the alternatives on offer. Religious and secular ideologies today no longer meet with disagreement as in the age of modernity, but rather with apathy and indifference. After all, contemporary "postmodern" cultural period is often defined as a period of "incredulity towards metanarratives", that is, of all-encompassing ideological interpretative frameworks, of "theories of everything"[49].

This feature of contemporary Czech culture, too, is something that Christians can basically agree with. Just as the Enlightenment was

---

[47] Cf. also D. Bosch, *Transforming Mission. Paradigm Shifts in Theology of Mission*, pp. 352-355.

[48] Cf. also D. Bosch, *Transforming Mission. Paradigm Shifts in Theology of Mission*, pp. 355-356.

[49] Cf. also D. Bosch, *Transforming Mission. Paradigm Shifts in Theology of Mission*, pp. 358-359.

evidently guilty of "the idolatry of reason", so more or less every ideology is guilty of the idolatrous overvaluing of a specific set of abstract assertions that it subsequently proclaims as "revealed truth" or "the inevitability of historical evolution" (as was the case with the communist ideology), to which everything and everybody must be subject[50].

In relation to the "post-ideological" character of contemporary culture it is becoming ever clearer that proclaiming the content of the Christian faith as a set of general assertions will find very few people who will listen to it in today's Czech society. By contrast, the fact that the core of the Christian faith and the Christian concept of God is not a system of dogmas, but a concrete story of a particular individual, is acquiring new relevance. The story of Jesus, from Bethlehem to Golgotha, his "life under the sign of faith, love, and hope", his "being there for others", can once again become a comprehensible starting-point for dialogue between believers and seekers. The concept of Christianity as "Jesus's radical humanism", and as the path toward "mature humanity" (Eph. 4:13) can in a similar sense be the starting-point for dialogue with the adherents of the contemporary forms of secular humanism.

To say the same thing from a different point of view: just as it has been evident in Czech cultural and religious history, the former connection between Church and state in the form of "Christendom" has lost all credibility and belongs irretrievably to the past, so it would seem that the concept of "Christianity" as a "worldview" (that is, one of the –isms of today's world) will not find a very large audience in contemporary Czech culture. By contrast, "Christianness", as a specific quality of life, as "being there for others" as Jesus was, as a life under the sign of faith, love, and hope, as the concrete implementation of the meaning of human existence in selfless and creative work for others – this has lost nothing of its comprehensibility and power of persuasion.

The Post-Individualistic Period

Contemporary Czech culture is also gradually moving to a *post-individualistic* stage. On the one hand it is true that recent cultural developments have not lead to a weakening of "European individualism". On the contrary, in a certain sense they strengthened it and brought it to a head. However, in so doing they also took it to its

---

[50] Cf. Francis, *Lumen Fidei*, par. 25 and 334, and especially *Evangelii Gaudium*, par. 61 and 231.

limits and revealed its pitfalls, which are becoming more and more obvious. For the individualism of contemporary Czech culture, characterised by "the idolatry of autonomous choice" and the freedom to shape one's identity out of various elements and components according to one's personal taste, and also by the temporary and conditional nature of all relationships and ties, is leading to an increase of loneliness of epidemic proportions. The divorce rate in Czech society is very high, a large part of the contemporary young generation has been raised in incomplete or dysfunctional families[51].

People are becoming increasingly free of the restricting ties of tradition, family, and all sorts of collectives, but at the same time they are (for the same reason) often becoming increasingly isolated. Indeed, even the astonishingly rapid development in the telecommunications field (from mobile phones to the social networks on the internet), paradoxically brings about restrictions in personal contacts between people, not mediated by the electronic media, and in spite of the increase in quantity of communication it may deepen the feelings of isolation and loneliness.

This is why in recent decades, in terms of the relative importance of factors making up people's individual identity, friendship with a number of "relevant others" has assumed considerable prominence. This becomes obvious particularly in comparison with the past, when factors such as family, local community, nation, and confessional and political affiliation were of fundamental importance in providing roots for one's identity[52]. As a result of the weakening of permanence of family relationships in recent decades and the loosening of ties with the communities of neighbourhood, town, nation, religion, and political parties, and also as a result of the decline in interest in public matters, one of the most important factors in forming contemporary Czech people's identity has become a "group of friends", which often functions as a new "adoptive family", which unlike a real family is not characterised by the inevitability of birth (you cannot choose your relatives), but by the freedom of mutual choice and shared values, interests, and tastes.

Just as Christians can essentially agree with the post-rationalist and post-ideological character of contemporary Czech culture, so they can welcome and appreciate its post-individualistic tendency from the

---

[51] Cf. J. Šiklová, "A Family Album: Changes of Family and the Present Time," in Z. Jurechová, P. Bargár (eds.), *Crisis Situations in the Czecho-Slovak Context after 1989*, pp. 146ff.

[52] Cf. L. Prudký, *Then and Now. Czech Society after 20 years*, pp. 108ff.

viewpoint of their faith[53]. The importance of interpersonal relationships, that is, the importance of the fact that human beings are social creatures and that relationships are a quintessential part of their make-up, is one of the most integral motifs of biblical faith and tradition. As is evident from the first chapters of the book of Genesis, people are only fully human in a network of relationships. There is no such thing as "private Christianity", divorced from the community of God's people[54].

The Church as a community, not just as an institution or an organisation, but as a tissue of interpersonal loving relationships, as a place of genuine encounter, can evidently offer contemporary people something that they are genuinely, and increasingly, looking for[55]. At any rate, in terms of the "success" of Christian mission in recent decades in the Czech Republic, the most common path to accepting faith has proved to be a prior phase of friendship with a Christian peer group. Conversion itself is usually preceeded by a lengthy period of attending various leisure activities, youth camps, and sporting or cultural activities organised by Christians, and not infrequently long before questions about faith and the meaning of life awaken in the individual in question.

In this respect, a new resonance can be found in the theological concept of the Church community as an "icon of the Trinity" or as a "living, pulsating image of Eternity", in other words as the presence on earth of a "heavenly quality", an essential dimension of which consists of human relationships[56].

The Post-Traditional Period

A further characteristic feature of contemporary Czech culture to which the dialogue between Christians and contemporary seekers can organically relate is the fact that many Czechs today have a very complicated and in fact to a certain extent "damaged" relationship to the past and to the future. In relation to the past it can be said that contemporary Czech culture is to a large degree *post-traditional*. The influence of tradition and its normative interpretation on private life and scale of values of individuals is declining. The "certainties handed down by tradition", which previously served as a support and anchor for the identity of individuals and whole communities, have simply failed to be

---

[53] Cf. D. Bosch, *Transforming Mission. Paradigm Shifts in Theology of Mission*, pp. 362ff.

[54] Cf. Benedict XVI., *Spe Salvi*, par. 13-15.

[55] Cf. Francis, *Evangelii Gaudium*, par. 67, 87 and 92.

[56] Cf. Benedict XVI., *Deus Charitas Est*, par. 19ff and especially Francis, *Lumen Fidei*, par. 45 and *Evangelii Gaudium*, par. 178.

passed on to the coming generation of Czechs. Most of the traditional respect to cultural past has in fact disappeared due to the disillusionment caused by the communist ideology and its abuse of power.

Tradition, the "tried and tested wisdom of our ancestors", thus no longer has that stabilising, and also supportive, meaning and function that it had in previous generations. The communist period has caused a large chasm of discontinuity with the cultural past[57]. The "life-giving link to tradition", to the important and meaningful story of the past, of which people felt they were a part and a continuation, and which provided them with orientation in life, goals, and motivation to overcome difficulties, can no longer fulfil that salutary function.

However, as a result of this "break with the past" many members of today's younger generation are experiencing a certain uprootedness. They do not feel connected to the cultural history of their ancestors. This state of affairs is increasingly being perceived as unsatisfactory. Sometimes the life-giving link to the great and powerful story of the past is missed so much that people "invent" it. Some contemporary Czech seekers are returning to their real or fictive "Celtic ancestors", to pagan Slavism or Teutonism, to shamanism, to a "close bond with Mother Nature", and so on. However, these returns to the past often have to work with fantasy, because frequently there is not enough reliable information about the past that they want to revive.

In this connection it is certainly worth mentioning the fact that an integral part of the Christian faith is and always has been a "life-giving link to a great and powerful story". The history of the people of God in biblical and post-biblical times including the rich cultural heritage of Christian Europe represents or could represent that great and powerful story that many contemporary Czechs lack. As is well known, Christians of past generations understood their own lives through reflecting on the stories of biblical heroes and important figures from the history of the Church, such as saints, martyrs, scholars and other heroes of Church history. Being rooted in this life-giving tradition, the "shared memory of the people of God", provided a crucial framework for their own self-understanding[58].

The fact that contemporary Czech culture is lacking in this link with tradition, and that it does not feel that it is part and continuation of a powerful and meaningful story, can once again be the starting-point for

---

[57] See for example V. Vaško, *She Was not Silenced. Chronicle of the Catholic Church in Czechoslovakia after the Second World War*, especially volume II.

[58] Cf. D. Hervieu-Léger's work *Religion as a Chain of Memory* (Cambridge: Polity Press, 2000).

dialogue between Christians and contemporary seekers. Furthermore, if we remember the oft-quoted observation that becoming a Christian means in an important sense "entering into a story", "finding oneself in the great narrative from Genesis to the book of Revelation", i.e. accepting the invitation into this story and adopting it as one's own "spiritual family tree" – then it would seem that Czech Christians are in a position to offer quite an interesting contribution to the discussion on the post-traditional nature of contemporary Czech culture. Something similar can be said about the relationship to the future.

The Post-Optimistic Period

Contemporary Czech culture is definitely in many respects a *post-optimistic* culture[59]. The Enlightenment optimism in relation to the future, shared and proclaimed by the architects of modernity is lost and beyond recovery[60]. The key word of the scientific and industrial revolution at the time when the Enlightenment was harvesting the wonderful fruits of its hard work was *progress*. This word had the status of a virtually indisputable dogma, especially in the Czech lands, which went through a very successful industrial revolution and became the economic heart of the Austrian Hungarian Empire. Progress "forward to happy tomorrows", to a gradual elimination of all the sources of poverty, deprivation and suffering, and to the establishment of a just society and universal prosperity, seemingly had no serious obstacle in its way, in the view of the majority of educated Czechs in the nineteenth century. However, a stop was put to this optimism by the series of tragedies of the twentieth century: Bolshevism in Russia, Nazism in Germany, and the First and Second World Wars, plus the misery of the forty years of communist regime.

What is more, the lessons learned and the consequences drawn from the horrific disasters of the twentieth century in no way remove the fears accompanying the view of the future. For the disillusionment with the Enlightenment optimism has been strengthened by further threats, whose removal is not in sight. Contemporary Czech politicians, philosophers, and other intellectuals (just as their colleagues in other countries) often struggle with a feeling of helplessness when they think about any long-term future perspective. They have little idea of how to deal with a number of "global time bombs" that hover like dark clouds

---

[59] See for example the subtitle of one of the most influential books by Tomáš Halík *The Paradoxes of Little Faith in a Post-optimistic Age* (*Paradoxy malé víry v postoptimistické době*) (Praha: Nakl. Lidové noviny, 2005).

[60] Cf. R. Tichý, M. Vávra, *Religion from a Different Angle*, p. 122.

on the horizon of the future. These include the fatal threats to the planet caused by the impact of the Western form of economy on the environment, the exhaustion of non-renewable resources in the all too foreseeable future, and the overpopulation of some parts of the planet, which furthermore are precisely those parts which have the lowest standard of living, which in view of the very unequal distribution of wealth means the threat of potential conflicts[61].

Just as we saw earlier in the case of the relationship with the past, in its relationship with the future, too, contemporary Czech culture is uncertain and in a certain sense "unhealthy". In its relationship to the past it is increasingly characterised by embarrassment or indifference, while in its relationship to the future it more and more often adopts a position of excluding and/or suppressing it. If an increasing number of contemporaries have not resolved satisfactorily either their relationship to the past or their relationship to the future, this inevitably strengthens an "orientation towards the present moment". The past is problematical, the future is problematical, and so all that remains is the present, which has to be filled with experiences, if possible right to the brim. Concentrating in this way on the present moment, on a kind of "eternal now" of enjoyment and amusement, it is possible to a certain extent to forget the problems of the past and the fears of the future. The orientation towards assembling and intensifying pleasant experiences, and the weakening of relationships to the past and the future, thus strengthen each other.

In this situation, Christians cannot, on the one hand, make light of the genuine threats and possible complications of future developments. On the other hand they are guided by their faith and their hope to the knowledge that all these phenomena and processes that may threaten the future of humankind on earth are not the final horizon[62]. Christians can rest assured that in spite of all appearances to the contrary this world and its future are in good hands. The answer to the anxious fears about the future is certainly not a cheap optimism, which disregards the seriousness of the situation, and even less one of ignoring them, but the justified hope which always was and is the "shared hope of the people of God". However, this shared hope is not simply some sort of internal state of mind. It is above all a motivation to take concrete steps, to a committed attempt to "put the world to rights", or, to put it more precisely, to implement the ideals and values of the Kingdom of God.

---

[61] Cf. D. Bosch, *Transforming Mission. Paradigm Shifts in Theology of Mission*, pp. 356-357, 361-362.
[62] Cf. Benedict XVI., *Spe Salvi*, par. 35.

In the Christian orientation towards life, this kind of "shared hope" in relationship to the future thus complements the "shared memory" in relationship to the past. The Christian relationship to both dimensions of time, past and future, can probably once again prove an interesting contribution to the discussion between Czech Christians and seekers on the post-traditional and post-optimistic nature of contemporary Czech culture.

The Post-Materialistic Period

As we have seen in the first part of this chapter, contemporary Czech culture is gradually becoming a more or less *post-materialistic* culture[63]. A multi-layered and far-reaching renaissance of spirituality is taking place, a search for the sacred dimension of reality, the discovery of the sacred as a welcome enrichment of life and a refreshing possibility to "discover the unknown and experiment with the mysterious". More and more often we find going hand in hand with this a rejection of simplistic atheism as something which is in fact quite "boring". Atheism celebrated its greatest success in the Czech lands in a period when it was surrounded by the aura of an emancipating movement, when it appealed to ardent idealistic hearts prepared to struggle to liberate Czech people from the domination of religious authoritarianism and "obscurantism and superstition". However, this struggle has long been over. The forty years of state imposed compulsory atheism proclaimed by the communist government did not really increase its popularity among Czech people. It is therefore no surprise that the number of those who proclaim their adherence to the fundamental principles of atheism have not increased in the last decades.

The freedom to experiment on the open field of spiritual experiences seems to be a far more interesting way for (especially young) people to amuse themselves and pass their free time than atheist indifference towards "the mysterious and the supernatural". In this connection, too, it is worth reflecting whether the Christian reaction to the renewed interest in all sorts of spiritual experience should not go beyond simply being indignant. Certainly it is not possible to uncritically agree with a consumer and "gourmet" approach to spiritual

---

[63] P. Fiala, *The Laboratory of Secularisation: Religion and Politics in a Non-religious Society: the Czech Case*, 93ff; Z. Nešpor, *Too Weak in Faith. Czech (Non)-religiosity in European Context*, pp. 106 and 161; M. Quesnell, *What Do We Think, What Do We Believe In and Who We Are*, pp. 170-171, and especially D. Hamplová, *Religion in Czech Society on the Treshhold of the Third Millenium*, pp. 15ff and 58ff.

experiences and experiments. On the other hand it is true that the changed cultural situation seems to encourage Czech Christians to find ways of offering and making accessible some of the treasures of the rich history of Christian spirituality to contemporary seekers.

The comments and observations made above provide (hopefully) just a handful of examples of promising themes, areas and issues that may inspire a potentially fruitful and mutually beneficial dialogue between Christians and contemporary Czech seekers. They also illustrate a certain way of attentive *discerning the signs of the times*, i.e. of a particular theological hermeneutics of contemporary Czech culture, guided by this biblical metaphor and the corresponding prophetic call of John XXIII, articulated in his constitution *Humanae Salutis* (quoted in the beginning of this chapter) by which he convoked the Second Vatican Council.

BIBLIOGRAPHY

Sources

Berger, P., Grace, D., Fokas, E. 2008. *Religious America, Secular Europe?* Ashgate, Burlington.
Fasora, L., Hanuš, J., Malíř, J. (eds.), 2007. *Sekularizace v českých zemích v letech 1848-1914 (Secularisation in Czech Lands between 1848 and 1914)*. Brno: CDK.
Fiala, J. 1997. *Hrozné doby protireformace (Horrible Times of Counter-Reformation)*. Heršpice: Eman.
Fiala, P. 2007. *Laboratoř sekularizace. Náboženství a politika v ne-náboženské společnosti: český příklad (The Laboratory of Secularisation: Religion and Politics in a Non-religious Society: the Czech Case)*. Brno: CDK.
Halík, T. 2005. *Noc zpovědníka. Paradoxy malé víry v postoptimistické době*. Praha: Nakl. Lidové noviny.
Hamplová, D. 2013. *Náboženství v české společnosti na prahu třetího tisíciletí (Religion in Czech Society on the Treshhold of the Third Millenium)*. Praha: Karolinum.
Hamplová, D. and Nešpor, Z. 2009. "Invisible Religion in a Non-believing Country: The Case of the Czech Republic." *Social Compass*. No. 56, 581-597.
Hanuš J. (ed.), 1999. *Náboženství v době společenských změn (Religion in the Time of Social Changes)*. Brno: Masarykova Univerzita.
Hervieu-Léger D. 2000. *Religion as a Chain of Memory*, Cambridge: Polity Press.
Lužný, D. and Navrátilová, J. 2001. "Religion and Secularisation in the Czech Republic." *Czech Sociological Review*. No. 9, 85-98.

Nešpor, Z. 2010. *Příliš slábi ve víře: Česká (ne)religiozita v evropském kontextu* (*Too weak in Faith. Czech (Non)-religiosity in European Context*). Praha: Kalich.

Nešpor, Z. 2006. "Tak zvaný český ateismus a jeho sociální a eklesiální dopady" (The so called Czech Atheism and Its Social and Ecclesial Consequences). In *Český ateismus. Příčiny, klady, zápory* (*Czech Atheism. Causes, Positives, Negatives*). Benešov: Eman.

Nešporová, O. and Nešpor, Z. 2009. "Religion: An Unsolved Problem for the Modern Czech Nation." *Czech Sociological Review*. No. 45, 1215-1237.

Prudký, L. (ed.), 2010. *Then and Now, Czech Society after 20 years*. Plzeň: Vyd. Aleš Čeněk.

Quesnell, M. 2002. *Co si myslíme, čemu věříme a kdo jsme* (*What Do We Think, What Do We Believe In and Who We Are*). Praha: Academia.

Sedláčková, M. 2011. "Trust and Democracy in the Czech Society." in Jurechová, Z. and Bargár, P. (eds.), *Crisis Situations in the Czecho-Slovak Context after 1989*. CECMS, Praha.

Spousta, J. 1999. "Czech Churches through the Eyes of Sociological Research." in Hanuš, J. (ed.). *Religion in the Time of Social Changes*. Brno: Masarykova Univerzita.

Štampach, I. 1999. "Náboženské spektrum České republiky" (Religious Spectrum of the Czech Republic). In Hanuš, J. (ed.), *Religion in the Time of Social Changes*. Brno: Masarykova Univerzita.

Tichý, R. and Vávra, M. 2012. *Náboženství z jiného úhlu* (*Religion from a Different Angle*). Brno: CDK.

Václavík, D. 2010. *Náboženství a moderní česká společnost* (*Religion and Modern Czech Society*). Praha: Grada.

Statistcs
   Czech Statistical Office www.czso.cz

Ecclesial Documents
   John XXIII., *Humanae Salutis*, 1961.
   Paul VI., *Evangelii Nuntiandi*, 1975.
   John Paul II., *Christifideles Laici*, 1988.
   John Paul II., *Centesimus Annus*, 1991.
   John Paul II., *Ut Unum Sint*, 1995.
   Benedict XVI., *Deus Charitas Est*, 2005.
   Benedict XVI., *Spe Salvi*, 2007.
   Benedict XVI., *Caritas in Veritate* 2009.
   Francis, *Lumen Fidei*, 2013.
   Francis, *Evangelii Gaudium*, 2013.

CHAPTER II

CATHOLIC CHURCH AND CZECH SOCIETY BEFORE AND AFTER THE FALL OF COMMUNISM

TOMÁŠ HALÍK

A spectre is haunting Europe – the spectre of communism, wrote Marx and Engels in the revolutionary year 1848. The spectre of Communism – one of the godless religions – fortunately ended its perambulation of Europe in the year 1989.

The half-century of Communist domination in Central and Eastern Europe can be divided into several phases. The first was the forcible Sovietization of those countries in the immediate post-war years up to the period of the 'unmasking of Stalin's personality cult' in the Soviet Union. The second starts after the expressions of popular protest against the Stalinist regimes – the 1953 uprising in East Germany, the 1956 Hungarian revolution and the victory of Gomulka's 'patriotic Communism' in Poland in October 1956 – and involved the establishment of bureaucratic state socialist regimes; it came to an end with the suppression of the Czechoslovak experiment with 'socialism with a human face', known as the Prague Spring, when the armies of the five Warsaw Pact countries invaded Czechoslovakia. The third phase was marked by the overall stagnation of the Soviet bloc during the rule of Leonid Brezhnev and ended with the creation of Solidarnosc in Poland in 1980. The fourth phase was Gorbachov's attempt to liberalize the Soviet regime known as 'perestroika', during the second half of the 1980s, which ended with the events in Central and Eastern Europe at the end of 1989 and the collapse of the Soviet Union.

Marxism was a kind of Christian heresy. Chesterton called heresy "truth gone mad", a particle of truth that wrenched itself loose from its context and expanded into dreadful dimensions. Marxism was a kind of inversion of Christian eschatology into the time-space of historical future, which can be planned and realized through revolutionary interventions into history. "We will order the wind, the rain, when it has to blow, to fall" went one of the songs of Communist youth.

Marxist ideology counted on religion dying away automatically in the moment when economic relations change because, according to Marx's teaching, religion was "nothing other than" superstructure and reflection of the class society, an expression of estrangement and the split personality of man. When the experiment of socializing the production processes came into force, the revolution in the superstructure did not take place. Christianity in Soviet Russia and later in its satellite states refused to die away. The violence that the communists started to use against Churches and believers was in fact proof that their theory failed in practice. Not even violence helped.

The most violent treatment of the Churches occurred prior to 1956. When the revolutionary terror of the 1950s exhausted itself and Communism grew older and fatter, the euphoria of one part of society and the fear and anger of the remaining part was replaced by general boredom. Two attempts to revise communist regimes – in 1956 and in 1968 – fell through. After 1968, in the majority of communist states, communist ideology changed into a curious type of state religion – nobody believed in it, not even its own high priests. Not even the vast majority of communist officials believed in Marxism – as a rule they were simply cynical apparatchiks. There were far less convinced Marxists in the East than in the West. Marxism had been dead in communist countries long before the fall of communism.

***

Czechoslovakia was the country where the Communists made their fiercest onslaught on the Churches and particularly on the Catholic Church. In the whole of Europe, perhaps only in Romania and Albania did Christians suffer even more drastic persecution at the hands of Marxist regimes. However, paradoxically that harsh treatment was partly counter-productive.

The Czech mentality contains a deep-seated sense of solidarity and sympathy with victims of injustice.

It is clear from memoirs published to date how great was the moral and psychological role played by priests imprisoned in Communist jails and labor camps. Thousands of the people who passed through the Stalinist prisons and concentration camps returned if not as converts then at least as sympathizers with enormous respect for the Church and the clergy. But for the persecuted Catholics those surroundings were also a school of tolerance and ecumenism: those who had previously moved in homogeneous Catholic surroundings met there with members of other Churches, as well as with proponents of Masarykian humanism, liberals, social democrats and even Communist intellectuals who had fallen foul of the regime – and they discovered that in spite of all the barriers, what united them was not just their harsh fate and resistance to the Communist dictatorship, but also a whole series of other values. That rapprochement continued into the seventies and eighties when many priests, who had returned from prison or on account of their over-enthusiastic ministry had lost their 'state consent for performance of pastoral duties', worked in manual jobs and there discovered forms of ministry akin to those of the French 'worker-priest' movement and made friends both with manual workers and with intellectuals who were banned from working in their professions.

A further chapter were the encounters of Catholics with other representatives of cultural and political dissent and cooperation with them in the seventies and eighties. The most celebrated platform for this was the Charter 77 movement, based on a manifesto published in January 1977 in response to the Helsinki Conference, where the countries of the Soviet bloc were obliged to formally recognize human rights documents and incorporate them in their legislation. The Charter was founded as a citizens' movement (chiefly intellectuals), whose aim was to make the regime respect its own legislation. The first group of several dozen signatories included two well-known Catholic theologians and several distinguished Catholic and Protestant lay people. When the regime responded to the initiative by persecuting the signatories, the Committee for the Defence of the Unjustly Prosecuted was set up and it started to deal with all the politically-motivated trials and regime harassment; the members of the Committee were soon to end up in prison themselves. They included two leading activists of the later Velvet Revolution: Václav Havel, now President of the Czech Republic, and Václav Malý, now auxiliary Bishop of Prague, as well as the lay Catholic philosopher and mathematician Václav Benda.

A specific role in the final period of Communism was played by the Czech primate, Cardinal František Tomášek, who had been one of the priests in the period around the Communist coup d'Etat in 1948 who secretly accepted ordination as a bishop on the Vatican's orders in the event that the existing bishops would be persecuted. When Archbishop Beran was released from internment in 1965 and sent into exile, the Communists chose Tomášek from among the existing bishops as being the 'softest' and most easily manipulated and gave him the job of Apostolic Administrator in Prague. For years it seemed that he would rather follow the Communists' orders, which was, however, in line with Vatican policy at the time: not to annoy the regime and avoid confrontation, as part of a policy of small steps toward improving Church-state relations. As late as 1977, Tomášek, in common with the other representatives of the Church issued a statement distancing himself from Charter 77. At that time Monsignor Tomášek was appointed Archbishop of Prague and Cardinal. Soon afterward an astonishing change came over that venerable priest, then in his eighties: the cautious bishop became the courageous cardinal and a symbol of resistance to Communist totalitarianism, recognized not only in his homeland and beyond the bounds of the Catholic Church, but also abroad.

Undoubtedly an important factor in this was the appointment of the new Pope who had no illusions about Communism. The Catholics in the whole soviet block received an enormous boost when the Cardinal of Kraków, Cardinal Karol Wojtyla was elected Pope in October 1978. The Polish Pope's first visit to his homeland in June 1979 demonstrated to the entire world the vitality of the Polish Church and the total failure of Communist ideology. The psychological atmosphere of that visit, which from a political perspective was a kind of maneuver of the opposition gave rise to the Solidarity movement. The creation of Solidarity meant for the history of Communism what the Battle of Stalingrad meant for Nazism.

John Paul II encouraged Cardinal Tomášek to adopt a more vigorous stance. The Cardinal surrounded himself with three advisors from the underground Church and started to make increasing overtures to the political dissidents. With the help of his advisors he began writing his letters to the government – later to become open letters – in which he defended not only persecuted Catholics but also all those denied civil liberties and human rights by the Communist regime. The mid-eighties also saw the emergence of a pastoral plan, drafted in underground Church circles, entitled 'The Decade of National Spiritual Renewal', certain aspects of which were reminiscent of Cardinal Wyszynski's project in connection with the millennium of Poland's conversion to Christianity. It was also advance preparation for the year 2000 and intended to be a laboratory of a new lifestyle for the coming millennium. The project was announced in a pastoral letter by Cardinal Tomášek which began with the stirring biblical words: 'Stand up and raise your heads!' and addressed not only to Catholics but to society as a whole. It was the time when Gorbachov's perestroika was getting under way and the authors of the project could sense that change was in the air. Their concern, however, was to stress that the healing of society could not be achieved merely by changes in external conditions, namely, changes in political and economic structures, but instead required changes in the entire social climate, changes of mentality and values, in ways of thinking and behavior.

The entire project was spread over a ten-year period. Each year was assigned a particular topic, inspired by one of the Ten Commandments which were interpreted from a positive angle. The commandment: 'Thou shalt not steal' inspired the topic: Work and Social Responsibility; the commandment: 'Thou shalt not commit adultery' gave rise to the topic Family Life, the commandment: 'Thou shalt not bear false witness' to the topic Truth and Justice, etc. In the second year of the project's implementation, there came the unexpectedly rapid and easy collapse of the Communist regime.

In the Czech lands, the events of November 1989 were heralded and colored by an ecclesiastical event that symbolized the major rapprochement between the Church and the nation at that time: just a few days before the student demonstration and the subsequent events that led to the fall of the Communist government, the Blessed Agnes of Bohemia was beatified in Rome in a ceremony attended by many Czech pilgrims and watched with enormous interest by the entire nation on television. During the days of the mass demonstrations, when the regime was deciding whether to capitulate or resort to military force, Cardinal Tomášek – during a mass in the Prague cathedral to give thanks for St. Agnes – spoke the following memorable words: 'At these important moments of the struggle for truth and justice in our country, I and the Catholic Church stand on the side of the nation!'

In the months that followed, complete scope for religious freedom opened up.

***

There is much talk in Eastern Europe about the need to "come to terms with the communist past" – and clearly that important task has yet to be fulfilled. Condemning communism is not simply a matter of bringing to trial a couple of communist criminals or distancing oneself verbally from the old regime and its ideology. It means pointing clearly to the "anthropological roots of totalitarianism", to those forms of behaviour and character traits that enabled the totalitarian regime to survive for so long.

In his celebrated essay "Power of the Powerless,"[1] written during the communist period, Václav Havel writes about a vegetable salesman who displays in his shop window – as was the custom in those days – a poster with Marx and Engels' slogan "Workers of the World, Unite!" to coincide with the anniversary of the Russian October Revolution. What did the vegetable salesman mean by his action? asked Havel. And there is his answer: The vegetable salesman didn't intend to proclaim anything about workers and their unity. What the vegetable salesman was saying to his superiors by the slogan placed among the onions and carrots was: I am a loyal citizen, not a troublemaker. Leave me in peace! I am one of those who regularly takes part in elections in which the Communist Party regularly receives its 99.9 percent of the votes. The regime can count on me when it needs to present the image of a unanimous and content mass of citizens.

In reality that was the secret of the communist regimes' stability. What kept communism in power was not belief in an ideology, or even the power based on the army and the police, but instead *an unwritten*

---

[1] Václav Havel, *The Power of the Powerless: Citizens Against the State in Central-Eastern Europe* (London: Hutchinson, 1985).

pact between the rulers and the ruled: if the ruled are apathetic to public life, if they played the game by the rules, then the regime wouldn't interfere too much in their private lives. The state would ensure the conforming citizens a certain degree of social security and would tolerate all sorts of things – poor working morale, petty everyday economic crime with respect to the "people's property", etc. That secret "social contract" bred an odd kind of human that the Russian writer Alexander Zinovjev and Polish philosopher, Fr. Tischner, dubbed "homo sovieticus"[2] – people devoid of initiative, creativity and responsibility.

In that atmosphere of constant mutual deception and fear, the only truly dangerous person was the one who, like the child in the story of the emperor's new clothes, unexpectedly stated the simple truth: that the emperor is naked. I can recall the liberating power of Havel's texts: here were words that revealed the true nature of our everyday reality, concealed behind propaganda Newspeak.

The game of subterfuge was disrupted by the fact that its unwritten rules were uncovered and described. Words received the power of light and became a weapon of light, of the power of the powerless.

***

According to opinion polls the Church achieved immediately after the fall of communism in the eyes of the Czech public an authority that it had clearly never enjoyed previously in modern history.

However, the situation began to change sharply in the following years: according to current opinion polls, fewer people in the Czech Republic than in any other European country – with the possible exception of the former GDR – acknowledge membership of the Church or a faith articulated through the Church.

I keep coming back to John Paul II.'s appeal to Czech Christians during his first visit in Prague in April, 1990: "You shall now build the temple of free life of your Church not by returning to what was here before you were robbed of your freedom. Build it in the strength of that to which you matured during persecution."

I hoped that those who went through the dark night of communism should by the power of their spiritual experience not only help build the temple of the Church, but also contribute in their part to the cultivation of a global civilization that is growing in place of the former bipolar world.

---

[2] Cf. Alexander Zinovjev, *Homo sovieticus* (Moscow 1991; in underground-press 1982) and Jozef Tischner, *Etyka solidarnosci oraz Homo sovieticus* (Kraków 1992).

But we must critically ask ourselves: To what have we matured? Suffering does not automatically help character to mature. It is not just necessary to "endure" pain, but also to make internal use of it. The experience of suffering can lead to re-evaluation of values in life and to higher sensibility towards the suffering of others – but the point is that this fruit of suffering should not just be a passing flash of lightning that we soon forget about and that we oust from our consciousness.

I feel anxious about how superficially most Christians from Central and Eastern Europe have dealt with the not-so-remote past, how little we have learned and how little we have contributed to entering this chapter of European history into the treasury of the historical experience of humankind.

Nonetheless it cannot be said that the Churches in those countries were indifferent to post-Vatican-II developments. In several papers I have tried to show that a number of Czech theologians during the period of severe persecution had reached conclusions similar to the Council on the basis of their own experience. The experience of shared suffering and struggle reconciled them with people of different political and religious persuasions, such as with Protestants, secular humanists, etc., and the prison experience led them to a vision of a Church free of all pomp and triumphalism, etc.

Even so, after the long years of isolation and persecution, the Church was in a fairly woeful state overall. Above all we lack a solid theology without which even the valuable experience of the difficult times will not be reflected upon. When certain representatives of east European Churches take pride in the fact that they lack "difficult" (nonconformist) theologians, it seems to me just as embarrassing as when someone boasts about having no tooth decay but omits to add that he has false teeth. Whenever sharp criticism of the West is voiced by people in those circles it is often based on prejudice, ignorance and misunderstanding, or on an unacknowledged inferiority complex. Many crisis phenomena that existed in the West arrive soon to postcommunist countries. Slogans like "*ex oriente lux – ex occidente luxus*" can arouse false hopes and have their origin in naiveté and self-deception.

The fact that relative poverty ruled in the East doesn't mean that poverty was regarded as a virtue in the spirit of the Gospel. It has only become a virtue since the return of freedom. The terrifying experience of the consumer society, coarse materialism, inadequate solidarity and the flouting of the elementary principles of fair play in the economic and political life of Eastern Europe are warning enough.

However, in this situation not even the Churches can assume the role of moralists, capable of themselves of achieving the moral renewal of society "off their own bat". The Church itself must undergo a process of renewal and repentance – and it would appear that the Churches show no more courage than the rest of society in this respect. The Churches in the communist countries were not solely made up of martyrs, they also included collaborators and compromisers – and those who were dissident in the days of communism can be just as bothersome now as they were then. It is certainly gratifying that in the post-communist world – either in society as a whole, or in the Churches – there has been no merciless retribution; nor has there been repentance – instead there has been a tendency to underplay and conceal guilt – and untreated wounds fester.

***

What was fatal for many liberal currents in the political and economic life of the post-Communist countries was the very fact that some representatives of those currents regarded liberalism as "Marxism in reverse". They inherited from Marxism a primitive economic determinism – what we used to call ironically "the fairy tale about the base and the superstructure". The Communists anticipated that changes in the economic base – the elimination of private ownership and the social ownership of the means of production – would automatically bring about changes within the cultural and spiritual "superstructure" and engender a "new Socialist man". Some representatives of economic liberalism in the post-Communist world – many of them convertees from Communism – anticipated, for their part, that the opposite changes in the economy, particularly the privatisation of industrial firms, would automatically alter people's attitudes and society's mentality, and that the "*homini sovietici*" would turn into people with all the "Protestant virtues" that Max Weber claimed were at the root of capitalism.

However it is easier to make soup out of fish than to turn fish soup back into fish again – the creation of a moral biosphere for a culture of democracy in the economy and politics of the post-Communist countries would seem to demand somewhat more profound changes and more complex nurturing than mere changes of ownership or economic relations.

Young democracies in post-communist countries – also in such countries that belonged to the most stable and solid European democracies between the World Wars, as did Czechoslovakia – still experience the distressful way through the desert. People are exposed to all kinds of temptations. I heard a story about Indians who were being removed by colonists from their original settlements and brought to new ones. Before the end of the trip, the Indians asked for a break, explaining: "Our bodies might be almost at the end of the trip, but our souls are still in those old homes. We have to wait for our souls".

Whenever I meet with various tokens of imperfection of the renewed democracies in Central and Eastern Europe, I remind myself of these words. We have to wait for our souls. But how long?

***

In the events of autumn 1989 the loser was communism. But it is very difficult to identify the victor. It certainly wasn't any of the forces within the communist-dominated societies (which is maybe one of the reasons why the populations of those countries don't seem to value freedom and democracy as much as one might have expected.) Liberation tended to come "from outside", rather than through their own endeavours, although it is certainly not our intention to disparage the suffering and heroism of the many opponents of communism.

The movements of dissidents were significant as a symbol of movement on the moral and cultural plane, but they were not the real political force that led the revolution. Within those movements various ideas were articulated which then became political programmes, and it was from those movements that emerged the personalities and groups that were to hasten the fall of the communist regimes and enable the rapid and non-violent transition of power. However that movement was not the actual author of political transformations: not only were the ordinary citizens taken by surprise by the rapidity and ease of the political changes but so also were most of the "opposition leaders". In the past such all-pervasive political changes tended to be the result of global, international or civil wars, or of uprisings headed by liberation movements. The "unbearable lightness" and "velvet nature" of the revolution in autumn 1989 make one even unsure to what extent it can be described as a revolution.

Casting my mind back it occurs to me that if there is a common denominator for what happened on the threshold of the nineteen nineties, then it is has to be the "process of globalisation" that knocked down the walls dividing Europe and swept the communist powers into the dustbin of history. We can even say, that the fall of communism was a side-effect of the globalisation process, the world-wide tide of economic integration and socio-cultural changes, in which regimes based on a rigid system of management were unable to stand the test.

The ruling circles of the communist regimes were neither willing nor able to communicate with their citizens and lost the power to control them. In a world of communication explosion it was impossible for them to keep their own citizens isolated within the ideological stereotypes of their own propaganda. The communist governments were unable to motivate their citizens in any way, having nothing to offer them either spiritually or materially. The countries of "real socialism" started to decline economically.

In the course of globalisation, problems arise that even Western democracy finds extremely hard to solve. Globalisation is a process that is not controlled by any governmental authority and it defies all political control. Attempts to create some kind of international authority to ensure a legal framework for mutual communication and help prevent and solve conflicts of interests between various groups have had only limited success.

There is even less reason to expect that some single religious or spiritual authority or institution will make any impression on the globalisation process. It is hard to guess what globalisation will bring in the field of religion. Which version of globalisation will triumph?

One of the fundamental issues of today's world in my view is whether, in the framework of the globalisation process, it will be possible to create a certain *culture of dialogue* and make globalisation a communication process. Inter-faith dialogue would be an inseparable part of such a process. Without it, global civilisation would simply be a new Tower of Babel.

I believe that in certain circumstances Catholicism could play an important role precisely in this area – it is able to lead a dialogue both with the world religions and with secular humanism, since it has points of contact with both of them. In his encyclical *Fides et ratio*, John Paul II called for a new alliance between faith, science and philosophy. During his long pontificate he supported interreligious dialogue.

With Pope Francis we stand again at the door-step of a new era. Many people in and outside the Church in the Czech Republic are following his new pastoral style, his new emphases and his reform initiatives and endeavors with great expectation, sympathy and hope. It will be very important for the future of the Church and also for the relation between Church and the Czech society, whether the new Pope becomes for our people only an icon for admiration or if his example will inspire and induce new spiritual energy among both Christians and "seekers".

BIBLIOGRAPHY

Havel, Václav. 1985. *The Power of the Powerless: Citizens Against the State in Central-Eastern Europe*. London: Hutchinson.
Tischner, Jozef. 1992. *Etyka solidarnosci oraz Homo sovieticus*. Kraków 1992.
Zinovjev, Alexander. 1991 [1982]. *Homo sovieticus*. Moscow.

CHAPTER III

EUROPE BETWEEN LAICITY AND CHRISTIANITY

TOMÁŠ HALÍK

Christianity engendered two unique, interlinked phenomena: the Church and secular culture. Similarly to the way that two parallel offshoots of the traditional religion of Israel emerged from its ruins after the destruction of the Jerusalem Temple, namely rabbinic Judaism and Christianity, so too, out of the ruins of mediaeval Christendom there grew more evidently than before *two branches* of its heritage: several varieties of modern ecclesiastical Christianity on the one hand, and "secular culture", on the other.

No religion, apart from Christianity, ever created a "Church" – an institution representing a specific religion as a whole, which, however, is not identical with the state or nation and which transcends cultural boundaries. The ecclesiastical form of Christianity explicitly professes its Christian faith and regards itself as its legitimate and exclusive institutional representation. The form of the Church, however, and its social role, have changed dramatically several times in the course of history.

The most striking change would seem to have occurred during the "papal revolution" of the Middle Ages, which had a decisive influence on the beginnings of secular culture. After the division of Western Christendom into Roman Catholic and Reformed wings, the emphasis on the "Church" in Christianity (particularly in Catholicism) became even stronger. At the same time "the Church" ceased to be an omnipresent fact of life and became a subject of discussion and reflection.

Secular culture – whose genealogy and historical transformations will be dealt with more fully later – is also a specific offshoot of the historical development of European Christianity, its unwanted progeny more precisely. The Church has often regarded it in the way that the elder son in Jesus' well-known parable regarded the younger or "prodigal" son. Should we too ask ourselves whether the time isn't ripe for the Church to change its attitude and instead perceive this "younger brother" with the eyes and heart of the wise and generous father from that parable?

If we are to understand Europe and modernity, we must study the history and present-day reality of those "two sons". It is my conviction that their capacity for mutual coexistence is the key to the future of Western civilisation as a whole.

It seems to me that this theme was increasingly of concern to Pope Benedict XVI in last years of his pontificate. As just one of many instances, I would cite what he said during his trip to Portugal: "In these centuries of a dialectic between enlightenment, secularism and faith, there were always individuals who sought to build bridges and create a dialogue, but unfortunately the prevailing tendency was one of opposition and mutual exclusion. Today we see that this very dialectic represents an opportunity and that we need to develop a synthesis and a forward-looking and profound dialogue. In the multicultural situation in which we all find ourselves, we see that if European culture were merely rationalist, it would lack a transcendent religious dimension, and not be able to enter into dialogue with the great cultures of humanity all of which have this transcendent religious dimension – which is a dimension of man himself.... So I would say that the presence of secularism is something normal, but the separation and the opposition between secularism and a culture of faith is something anomalous and must be transcended. The great challenge of the present moment is for the two to come together, and in this way to discover their true identity. This, as I have said, is Europe's mission and mankind's need in our history."

When we contemplate the history of secularisation, probably the earliest roots are to be found in two important features of the Bible's attitude to the world. I have in mind "the demagnification of nature" in the biblical concept of creation (distinguishing between the Creator God and creation), and also the "desacralisation of political power", as we find it in the therapy of the exodus (the rebellion against the "divine pharaoh") and in the prophetic critiques of holders of political power. That line of criticism runs from Nathan's critique of King David and Jesus' dialogue with Pilate, through the entire history of Christianity up to and including the martyrs of conscience of the twentieth century's totalitarian regimes. (One must heed God more than people; God's kingdom is not of this world – albeit the very idea of God's kingdom holds up a critical mirror to this world.)

Crucial in the differentiation of Church and secular society were the relations between the papacy and the empire that culminated in the investiture dispute between imperial and papal power at the height of the Middle Ages. The "papal revolution", which occurred at that time, sometimes referred to as the "first European revolution" broke the monopoly of imperial power and helped bring into being the secular state and secular culture. The European West (unlike Byzantium) became a two-dimensional, bi-polar society. Some authors (e.g. Zakaria[1]) regard that to be a fundamental turning-point in the Western history of freedom. (According to Hannah Arendt, the mediaeval differentiation of the roles of Pope and Emperor was analogous to the division of *power* and *authority* between emperor and senate in Ancient Rome.[2])

As stated earlier, that conflict between empire and papacy also had a major influence on the form of the Church and its social, political and cultural roles in later centuries. Unlike anywhere else on earth there was created a division of power on a single territory, the coexistence of two powers (ecclesiastical and secular), which, for a long time, were effectively complementary.[3] This is because everything was bound together by *Christianity as a religion*. Here I am using the term religion solely in the sense of sociological functionalism – religion as an integrating social force, as a "common language" – whatever holds society together is its *religion* (religio).

In the period between the emperors Constantine and Charlemagne, Christianity assumed the form of a "religion" and it lasted to the beginning of modern times. In the course of modern times, however, Christianity lost that political and cultural function, ceasing to be a "religion" in that sociological sense of the word. Marcel Gauchet wrote that Christianity was the religion that would surpass religion "*la religion de la sortie de la religion*") – that it would gradually abandon its political role and move out of the infrastructure of society into its superstructure, i.e. into the realm of culture.[4]

Christianity allowed itself to be manipulated into the role of *world view/ Weltanschaung* (the basis of which was the long-standing tendency to regard faith as "conviction"). In a period of plurality of opinions, that role is greatly undermined, however, which is why traditional Christianity and its claim to universality finds itself in crisis. P.L. Berger suggests that the popular though ambiguous and problematic term "secularisation" be supplanted by the term (or paradigm): *pluralisation*.[5]

---

[1] Cf. Fareed Zakaria, *The Future of Freedom: Illiberal Democracy at Home and Abroad* (W.W. Norton & Company, 2003).

[2] Cf. Hannah Arendt, *Between Past and Future: Six exercises in political thought* (New York: Viking, 1961).

[3] Cf. Franz X. Kaufmann, *Kirchenkrise – Wie überlebt das Christentum?* (Freiburg i. Br.: Herder, 2011).

[4] Cf. Marcel Gauchet, *Le désenchantement du monde. Une histoire politique de la religion* (Paris: Gallimard, 1985).

[5] Cf. Peter L. Berger, *A far glory: the quest for faith in an age of credulity* (New York: The Free Press, 1992).

Various phenomena subsequently sought to play religion's integrative role as a "common language" and social cement: initially, *natural science* and later *culture and art* (particularly during the Romantic era); in the 19th century it was often *nationalism* and *"political religion"*: the ideologies and eschatologies of totalitarian movements such as Nazism and Communism. Nowadays religion's sociological role as a universal cement is played by the *market, the capitalist economy*, and particularly the most important market, the information market – of which the *mass media* are a case in point. The media have been most effective in taking over religion's social role – they interpret the world and are arbiters of what is true and of importance: they offer big symbols and stories that shape the lifestyles and thinking of millions of people. It strikes me that one could describe the contemporary media in the sociological sense as "the religion of the present-day West".

The fact that traditional ecclesiastical Christianity lost the role of "religion" in the course of modern times would seem to represent an irreversible change. A crucial factor in that process was most likely the division of Western Christianity and the subsequent religious wars of the 17th century. In reaction to that event there emerged a significant movement among European intellectuals who were disgusted by both warring camps, the Catholics and Protestants, (from Erasmus, say, to Hobbes and Locke) that initially strove for a "third path" for Christianity. Eventually it gave rise to the Enlightenment and gradually moved further away from traditional ecclesiastical Christianity, so that it even clashed with it sharply on many occasions.

In addition to the division of Western Christianity into Catholic and Protestant there has also been a schism of a more fateful kind. The ecclesiastical and "secular" forms of Christianity ceased to be complementary and their representatives ceased to understand each other, increasingly forming themselves into opposing camps. In the period when the mouthpieces of that "secular tendency" were Enlightenment intellectuals and scholars, that intellectual current often abandoned the fundamental pillar of Christian identity: faith was supplanted by secular rationalism. (In his important work "A Secular Age", Charles Taylor traces the gradual shift from Christian faith to deism and thence to "exclusive humanism".[6]) This "exclusive humanism" could be called *secularism*. (The term "secularisation" often denotes a historical process, whereas "secularism" describes an ideology that interprets this process as necessary, irreversible and desirable

---

[6] Cf. Charles Taylor, *A Secular Age* (Cambridge: Harvard University Press, 2007).

progress from "religious superstition" to a "bright future under the aegis of reason and science". Secularism takes various forms and is sometimes allied to militant atheism).

Without doubt the cultural and political triumph of secularity among European intellectuals in the 18th century was partly due to the fact that its power rested on what was then the "religion of the modern age": modern natural science, which replaced theology as the dominant language of the modern elite and the arbiter of truth. Furthermore its effective offspring, modern technology, started to radically transform the world. Then, in the technological world of the 19th and 20th centuries, whole strata of the population started to turn away from traditional ecclesiastical Christianity, starting with the world of labour (which was, moreover, wooed by the "political religions" referred to earlier, particularly socialist eschatology).

Ecclesiastical Christianity reacted to the victory of secularism in two unfortunate ways – either *liberalism*: uncritically allowing its identity to dissolve into the secular culture, or *fundamentalism*, withdrawing into a ghetto of disgruntled and paranoid "counter-culture". (The classic example of the latter was the notorious anti-modernist struggle in Catholicism at the turn of the 20th century; anxiety over lost positions in politics and culture and the loss of intellectual elites did not lead the Church establishment to seek self-critically the real reasons for the situation, but instead to indulge in a paranoid "witch-hunt", whereby the Church lost many of its creative spirits as a result of intimidation, persecution, impoverishment and psychological pressure, and to a large degree it castrated itself intellectually. That self-destructive tendency, which would have gradually turned the Church into an obscurantist sect on the fringe of society, was not halted until the 2nd Vatican Council.)

However, secularism's cultural and political victory conceals a temptation for secularism to become a "religion" of sorts, and, moreover, a religion with very intolerant and totalitarian features.

The present-day dilemma of secular culture and society resides in whether it is to be a "healthy secularism" or become one of the militant variety. Christians in the Central and East Europe are familiar with the face of militant secularism in its "hard form" of the persecution of Churches under the Communist regimes. There is also its "soft form" in the West: attempts to marginalising Christianity in the name of the ideology of multiculturalism and political correctness.

If the Christian component of European culture disappears, that culture will not become atheistic (in the sense of religion-free), but "religious" (or pseudo-religious), i.e. religious in a non-Christian (and often anti-Christian sense). Indeed even its atheism will then become a kind of "religion", or even a "state religion", as witnessed in the countries of the Soviet bloc.

I said that Christianity would seem to have lost for good the role of *religion* in the sense of a common language for this cultural area. But the role of Christianity as a "world view" has also been undermined – precisely at a time when there is talk of a global return or revival of religion and of the emergence of an abundant global "market of religions". Could Christians be content with the fact that Christianity is regarded as one of thousands of "world views" on today's market of ideas and religions, on which cheap exotic goods are in much greater demand, anyway?

What will be Christianity's future role in a society where "secular culture" will have forced the ecclesiastical form of faith onto the fringes of society, among "interest groups", and in which "the pursuit of faith" will be regarded as a private free-time activity – as a private "hobby"?

Outside Europe there are attempts to *transform Christianity into a political ideology* – we recall the radical left-wing variants in some currents of liberation theology, and we have also been witnessing the opposite extreme, the Religious Right on the right wing of American politics. In Europe there is no real likelihood of Christianity being turned into a political instrument. Latin-American liberation theology was attractive for the liberal Christian left in the West, but it came to an end with the fall of the Marxist regimes in Europe. In certain parts of Europe (such as Poland, Norway or Belgium), some political groups attempt to link Christian symbols and rhetoric with nationalism, xenophobia, anti-Semitism, using fear of immigrants, Islam and the liberal policies of the EU, etc. Crises of democracy could enable these hitherto extreme fundamentalist and populist circles to gain greater influence. Christians will undoubtedly continue to involve themselves in political life, and no doubt also across the entire political spectrum; but it looks as if the notion of "Christian politics" is a thing of the past in Europe.

So far there have been two relatively successful attempts at transforming traditional Christianity. The first is a reaction to the evident decrease in the numbers of "dwellers" and an increase in the numbers of "seekers", to the shift "from religion to spirituality", and to the growing tendency of "believing without belonging" – it is a renunciation of the classic parochial form of religious life and the offer of opportunities to discover emotional religious experience. In some of the "new movements" in the Church, particularly the "charismatic movements", we can encounter a pietism that does not make great demands on those who take part in small groups or large rallies at sports stadiums, but one can also find very exclusive groups that offer their members – particularly at a time when family life is in crisis – a "substitute family" and a firm identity. Sometimes such attempts at responding to this longing for spirituality by developing the *mystical and meditative traditions of Christianity* have no qualms in enriching those traditions with elements borrowed from the religions of the Far East.

Another successful approach (i.e. one that is relatively acceptable to the majority secular society) has been attempts to present the Church as *an expert on moral problems* (so long as it does not consist of vacuous moralising and an excessive emphasis on sexual ethics, but instead on the ethics of science, economy, politics and media). Where the Church disposes of qualified experts, the latter are welcome in the media and on consultative bodies of political institutions as an important voice in current debates.

The great Western "cultural revolution" of the 1960s (that "second Enlightenment") engendered a chronic crisis of confidence in traditional institutions, and with it a radical change in the relationship of most Christians to their own Church. In one country after another the homogenous Catholic social and cultural framework disintegrated (in Quebec in the 1960s, Germany between 1968 and 1978, later in Italy and Spain, and most recently in Ireland, and it looks as if the process has already started in Poland too). The Churches (but also the political parties and trade unions) are ceasing to play the role of institutions with which entire sectors have traditionally fully identified, and are beginning to be perceived as firms providing certain services and offering a range of goods that people can select from as they fancy. Whereas until some time ago it looked as if those services offered by religious institutions would be displaced by the competition from secular institutions, it would now seem that even in highly secularised societies the Churches are irreplaceable in certain spheres of life and at certain moments of history (Even many "non-religious" people, not to mention a considerable number of convinced atheists, demand the Church's assistance for christenings, weddings and burials. The Churches are packed on such occasions as the death of Princess Diana or 11th September 2001; and psychologists have not displaced chaplains from armies, prisons or hospitals.)

These days sociologists often maintain that the "secularisation hypothesis" is too out-dated and controversial to be used as a hermeneutical key to understanding the role of religion in today's world. Secularisation has turned out to be neither a universal nor an irreversible phenomenon, as it once seemed. The secularisation process can only be observed in certain cultures, and it involves only some sections of the population, and, in particular, only some forms of religious life. The generalised extinction of religion is out of the question. The revitalisation of certain classical religions, the repoliticisation of monotheistic religions in the last quarter of the 20th century, the boom in new forms of religiosity and new religious movements and cults, the revived interest in spiritual values, the fundamentalist or syncretic reactions of religions to the globalisation process, the revival of religion in many countries after decades of persecution, the prevalence of "pseudo-religious" and "crypto-religious" elements in secular culture – all these factors have led present-day sociologists to adopt the view that it is necessary to talk in terms of a transformation of the forms of religion and not about its extinction.

If the Enlightenment thinkers who were expecting the extinction of religion were around nowadays, they would see the end of the "religion" that they themselves "constructed": namely, a specific area of reality separate from other areas of culture. In that Enlightenment sense – which is unparalleled both in the earlier tradition and in non-European cultures, which have difficulties even with the very notion of "religion" – "religion" truly is in decline in the West. If religious institutions concentrate solely on that type of religion, and that applies to many ecclesiastical forms of modern times, they are indeed in profound crisis.

However, those things, which for centuries were fundamentally associated with religion: spirituality, many spiritual and moral values, faith, hope, love, the struggle with selfishness and idolatry, the quest for communication with the transcendent dimension of reality and the ultimate concern of life – do not automatically disappear along with certain traditional forms of religion. Rather they "overflow" into other forms, whether in the institutional or intellectual sense – into another kind of language and expression. They are articulated differently.

The history of religion in Europe is by no means at an end, as certain zealous apostles of atheism predicted. It is a continuing drama, full of reversals and surprises. I am convinced that that story of Christianity, which some years ago entered the third millennium of its existence, will continue to be a thrilling one, both in Europe and elsewhere.

BIBLIOGRAPHY

Arendt, Hannah. 1961. *Between Past and Future: Six exercises in political though* (New York: Viking.
Berger, Peter L. 1992. *A far glory: the quest for faith in an age of credulity*. New York: The Free Press.
Gauchet, Marcel. 1985. *Le désenchantement du monde. Une histoire politique de la religion*. Paris: Gallimard.
Kaufmann, Franz X. 2011. *Kirchenkrise – Wie überlebt das Christentum?* Freiburg i. Br.: Herder.
Taylor, Charles. 2007. *A Secular Age*. Cambridge: Harvard University Press.

Zakaria, Fareed. 2003. *The Future of Freedom: Illiberal Democracy at Home and Abroad.* W.W. Norton & Company.

CHAPTER IV

"THE MYTH OF THE 'NONRELIGIOUS AGE'"[1]
A SOCIOCULTURAL TRANSFORMATION OF RELIGION IN MODERNITY

PAVEL ROUBÍK

People who were satisfied with being blessed by the Church – such people are no longer here. Johann Salomo Semler (1786)

INTRODUCTION

The transition to modernity[2] is commonly deemed to be "the profoundest break in the history of Christianity."[3] The religious-cultural developments in modernity offer an uneven picture. The most noticeable finding of social statistics is doubtlessly the decreased ecclesiality of broad sections of Western population as a visible behavioural change related to religious participation in societies shaped by Christianity. It has brought about significant side-effects for the tradition of religious memory, for religious socialization and for public communication.[4] Of course, if we look at the processes of rechristianization in North America, the booms of Pentecostal Christianity in Latin America and Africa, the growth rate of Christianity in Korea and recently in China, the expectations of social integration in relation to the Orthodox Church in post-communist Russia and the anti-capitalist symbolism of the Holy See now, the strongly secularized Western and Central Europe seems to be an exception rather than a rule in the relation between (Christian)

---

[1] Gottfried Sprondel, "Die Legende vom 'religionslosen Zeitalter'. Auch in der nachchristlichen Wirklichkeit wird nach Gottgefragt," *Lutherische Monatshefte*, 24 (1985), pp. 557-561.

[2] The question, which is not necessarily unimportant, how many modernities there are, should be only mentioned.

[3] Jörg Lauster, *Religion als Lebensdeutung: Theologische Hermeneutik heute* (Darmstadt: Wissenschaftliche Buchgesellschaft, 2005), p. 148.

[4] Cf. Jörg Dierken, *Fortschritte in der Geschichte der Religion? Aneignungeiner Denkfigur der Aufklärung*, ThLZ.F 24 (Leipzig: Evangelische Verlagsanstalt, 2012), pp. 230-231.

religion and society today.[5] At the same time, despite religious efforts which counteract the secularized culture, i.e. the various kinds of the so-called "return of religion", we cannot speak about any empirically demonstrable end of secularization.[6] But there is no question that in contemporary European societies, religion, this "oldest and deepest" "social force,"[7] plays an important role in the actual search for the "essentials" of the Western culture. As an example of this fact we can mention the so called bio-political discussion, which was perceived as a sort of "Kulturkampf" between the Christian and the scientistic understanding of human being.[8] If Europe is "based on equal secular values",[9] which were repeatedly referred to as an argument for or against the admittance of Turkey to the European Union, the word "secular" must actually mean "post-secular"[10] in this context, i.e. values, admittedly derived from Christianity. The list of indications displaying the presence of religion in the secular culture would be long.

The term "secularization" (*Verweltlichung*) in its contemporary – metaphorical (!) and not only historically-descriptive but also ideologically-political[11] – use in social sciences as a category of description and interpretation comes from German Historicism of the outgoing 19th century. With this term, Wilhelm Dilthey, Ernst Troetsch and Max Weber wanted to explain the complexities of modern consciousness and its specific differences in comparison with the pre-modern consciousness. The term of secularization has become a methodical instrument of cultural-hermeneutic analyses.

---

[5] Cf. Hartmut Lehmann, "Ein europäischer Sonderweg in Sachen Religion," in *Europäische Religionsgeschichte. Ein mehrfacher Pluralismus* I, Hans G. Kippenberg, Jörg Rüpke and Kocku von Stuckrad (eds.), (Göttingen: Vandenhoeck & Ruprecht 2009), pp. 39-59.

[6] Cf. Jörg Dierken, *Selbstbewußtsein individueller Freiheit. Religionstheoretische Erkundungen in protestantischer Perspektive* (Tübingen: Mohr Siebeck, 2005), p. 49.

[7] Jan Sokol, "Politika a náboženství," in *Demokracie a ústavnost*, Jan Kunc (ed.), (Prague: Karolinum, 1999), pp. 232-237; here p. 233.

[8] So Wolfgang Frühwald, "Der optimierte Mensch," *Forschung & Lehre*, 8 (2001), pp. 402-405.

[9] Cf. "Europa basiert auf gleichen säkularen Werten: Drei Fragen an Meliha Benli Altunisik", this interview is available online, see: http://www.bpb.de/internationales/europa/tuerkei-und-eu/52317/meliha-benli-altunisik [August 21, 2014].

[10] Cf. Jürgen Habermas, *Glauben und Wissen* (Frankfurt a. M.: Buchhändler-Vereinigung, 2001).

[11] Cf. Hartmut Lübbe, *Säkularisierung. Geschichte eines ideenpolitischen Begriffs* (Freiburg/München: Alber, 1965).

"Secularization is a category of the self-awareness of modernity concerning the religious conditions of its origin." This is the sentence with which Ulrich Barth, one of the most important contemporary German-speaking theologians, begins his penetrating chapter about secularization.[12] The reflection of secularization presented in this chapter is to a large degree influenced by his thought. It tries to ask the question of secularization in an interdisciplinary way, i.e. hopefully without any "methodological reductionism"[13], assessing it from the viewpoint of the *religious subject*. It focuses particularly on the sociocultural transformation of religion with regard to transformation processes in the religious self-awareness of human beings. Unfortunately, I cannot really make much use of the discussion about secularization among Czech Protestant theologians and philosophers, because their approach to this topic has been influenced to a large degree by the "secularization paradigm" and also by the one-sided inclinations to follow the theology of Karl Barth and Dietrich Bonhoeffer, thereby tending towards a theological anti-psychologism and groundless anti-liberal attacks. Religion became almost a swear word – oftentimes a synonym for superstition, a sign of immaturity or even of sinfulness. Under the cloak of secularization, they actually preached and taught a sort of "secularism".[14] Not only Schleiermacher and Troeltsch but also

---

[12] Ulrich Barth, "Säkularisierung und Moderne. Die soziokulturelle Transformation der Religion," in *Religion in der Moderne* (Tübingen: Mohr Siebeck, 2003), pp. 127-165; p. here 127.

[13] Pavel Hošek, "Prolegomena k interdisciplinárnímu tázání po vztahu evropské sekularity a západního křesťanství," *Sociální studia* 3-4 (2008), pp. 15-26; here p. 16.

[14] Josef L. Hromádka, the most prominent Czech Protestant theologian of the post-World war II era, wrote: Secularization has become "a program of the new social and culture development." All religious processes are only a sort of "scenery". We cannot go before the process of secularization neither before 1918 or 1938. Religion is "a self-divinization or... self-alienation and self-illusion," even "idolatry and superstition". Josef L. Hromádka, *Evangelium o cestě za člověkem. Úvod do studia Písem a církevních vyznání* (Prague: Kalich, 1958), 306.307. For the Protestant philosopher Ladislav Hejdánek religion undergoes an internal decline; "it becomes an alien element in modern society, it becomes an anachronism and an obstacle. Secularization means not only decline of religion but also and primarily criticism of religion. The modern human being... is not a religious sceptic but an opponent of religion... Secularization has become a program that has to be finished." Ladislav Hejdánek, "Víra v sekularizovaném světě" (1962), in *Filosofie a víra. Nepředmětnost v myšlení a ve skutečnosti* II (Prague: OIKOYMENH, 1999), pp. 26-34; here p. 26. "The world has become an infection of religiosity, the

Bultmann and Tillich were stigmatized as "liberals". Nonetheless, as some writings of the younger theological generation show, the tendency to distinguish between "good" and "bad" theology (using a positive evaluation of secularization as a criterion), thank God, fades.

In the first part of this chapter, I deal with the sociological model of secularization, in the second part I focus on the question of the relationship between secularization and the Enlightenment, and in the third part, which is the most important one, I try to analyse the crisis of religion employing the very notion of secularization.

A LIMITED APPLICABILITY OF THE SOCIOLOGICAL MODEL OF SECULARIZATION

The extraordinary merit of recent sociology of religion consists primarily of creating conceptual instruments which enable us to describe secularization in a much less biased way than was possible within the framework of theological discussions.[15] Thanks to the far-reaching sociological analyses of secularization the specific profile of modernity can be demonstrated much more vividly. This contribution, however, has come at the cost of the sociological overload of religion.[16] Already the founders of sociology – Emile Durkheim and Max Weber – attributed to religion a fundamental role in integrating societies and constituting value-oriented lifestyle and, accordingly, they viewed

---

religious epidemics ends at least in some parts of the world". Ladislav Hejdánek, "Ještě křesťanství a náboženství" (1966), in *Filosofie a víra*, pp. 53-56; here p. 55. Human beings should break free from religion because of the Christian faith. "Christianity is in its core no religion...." Ladislav Hejdánek, *Úvod do filosofování*, Part 4 (1971) (Prague: OIKOYMENH, 2012), pp. 64-78; here p. 77. Josef Smolík, the long-time professor of practical theology at the Protestant theological faculty in Prague, noticed an increasing religiosity which is "a guilt of the Church". It requires "a penitent confession" because "the real experienced Gospel eliminates religion" and it leads to "a form of secularization." Josef Smolík, "Poznámky k elaborátu J. Ellula," *Křesťanská revue*, 40 (1973), p. 93.

[15] Cf. Barth, "Säkularisierung und Moderne," p. 156.

[16] This finding does not apply to Hans Joas who, in his works on religion, proves to be an excellent philosopher as well. Cf. Hans Joas, *Braucht der Mensch Religion? Über Erfahrungen der Selbsttranszendenz* (Freiburg/Basel/Wien: Herder, 2004) (in Engl. *Do We Need Religion? On the Experience of Self-Transcendence* [Boulder: Paradigm Publishers, 2009]; *Glaube als Option. Zukunftsmöglichkeiten des Christentums* (Freiburg: Herder, 2012).

sociology of religion as the key discipline of sociology.[17] It may sound nice for theologians and philosophers of religion but it is ambiguous.

From the sociological point of view, the flagrant decrease of ecclesiality means primarily a deep transformation of religious forms, whereas religious contents remain more or less constant. Secularization is understood as "a process of evolutionary differentiation of societies into functionally independent segments."[18] This brings about "deinstitutionalization, deconfessionalization, pluralization, dedogmatization and individualization of religious attitudes".[19] Such a conception of secularization assumes the evolutionary theory of history. According to this model, the general development of humankind has proceeded towards a sort of institutional structuring in which the "profane" domain emancipates itself from the "sacred" one. Modern society is a socially differentiated society. Secularization means an evolutionary process culminating in the appearance of fully differentiated societies.[20] However, this explanatory model must be deconstructed. The essence of modernity can be seen – with Max Weber – not in the process of functional differentiation itself but in the enormous increase of rationalisation in the functionally differentiated spheres. The process of social differentiation may well be a consequence of religious neutrality of the extra-religious social subsystems – and not necessarily vice versa as the evolutionary model of secularization would suggest.[21] One does not need to find a definite answer because these two situations could be understood as a result of an interactive process with the same precondition, namely the existence of comprehensive orders accepted by the society as a whole – including their institutional enforcement. This ideological consensus broke down at first in the religious field. Mutually competing religious systems found themselves in competition with the religiously neutral subsystems of society (politics, economy or science) with their own functional logic. Therefore, the denominationalization in the 16th and 17th century was one of the most significant factors which contributed to secularization.[22]

---

[17] Cf. Barth, "Säkularisierung und Moderne," p. 158.
[18] Barth, "Säkularisierung und Moderne," p. 158.
[19] Barth, "Säkularisierung und Moderne," p. 158.
[20] Cf. Barth, "Säkularisierung und Moderne," p. 161.
[21] Cf. Wolfhart Pannenberg, *Anthropologie in theologischer Perspektive* (Göttingen: Vandenhoeck & Ruprecht, 1983), pp. 161-162.
[22] Cf. Barth, "Säkularisierung und Moderne," pp. 162-163 and the confrontation of Wolfhart Pannenberg with Hans Blumenberg in Pannenberg's book *Gottesgedanke und menschliche Freiheit* (Göttingen: Vandenhoeck & Ruprecht, 1972), pp. 5.126-127.

The comprehensive explanatory power of the sociological model of secularization is based on the presumption that religion "plays a major role in relation to the ideal organization of meaning."[23] Social and individual questions of meaning and religious questions are certainly not two different domains but they cannot be simply identified. The former need not to reach the latter. There are actually not three[24] but only one transcendence which may be (and – as we believers confess – wants to be) experienced as an absolute, "wholly other" dimension of reality – and of meaning. Such experience – or, to use Schleiermacher's expression, "the sense and taste for the infinite"[25] – is what we call religion. "Using religion for anything finite contradicts it."[26]

Religion does not limit itself to the traditional manifestations of holiness, whether of institutional or non-institutional kind. Along with its role for orientation, ritualization and sacralisation on the collective level, religion also includes analogous processes within religious consciousness. However, trying to identify alternative phenomena, which would be functionally equivalent to explicitly religious forms, is not without ambiguities. The breadth to which the term "religion" has been expanded through sociological discourse – from certain political engagements to willingness to contribute donations for charity projects, from rituals of personal care to worshipping national ice hockey team – is confusing: almost anything may be viewed as suspiciously (pseudo/crypto/para) religious. But can religious attitudes be adequately understood just from their external aspects? We have to presuppose an affirmative answer to this question if we want to take seriously not just one's conscious and explicit religiousness but also her or his implicit and or opaque religiousness which is no less problematic for psychology of religion than the distinction between sacred and profane domain is for the sociology of religion.[27]

---

[23] Barth, "Säkularisierung und Moderne," p. 160.

[24] So Thomas Luckmann, "The New and the Old in Religion," in Pierre Bourdieu and James S. Coleman (eds.), *Social Theory for a Changing Society* (Boulder/San Francisco/Oxford: Westview, 1991), pp. 167-188.

[25] Friedrich D. E. Schleiermacher, *Über die Religion. Reden and die Gebildeten unter ihren Verächtern* (1799), § 52, in *Kritische Gesamtausgabe* I/2: *Schriften aus der Berliner Zeit 1769-1799*, Günter Meckenstock (ed.) (Berlin: Walter de Gruyter, 1984), p. 212.

[26] Dierken, *Selbstbewußtsein individueller Freiheit*, p. 57.

[27] Cf. Barth, "Säkularisierung und Moderne," pp. 160-161.

SECULARIZATION AND THE ENLIGHTENMENT

Ulrich Barth vigorously opposes both the widespread conviction that there is a direct interconnection between secularization and the Enlightenment[28] and the simplistic identification of modern times with dechristianization.[29] We find this – even empirically questionable – conviction already in Friedrich Gogarten: "...the profaning Enlightenment claims that there is no binding order anymore since the time when Logos removed all the mythic powers."[30] The so called enlightenment freedom culminates in "the original disobedience which equals disbelief" and it "rebels against the constitutional order of all being; against the order that God is God and human is human."[31] Barth summarizes: The Enlightenment "can barely be taken as the source of a cultural decline, the motor of the dechristianization or the origin of a world without God".[32]

Which methodical criteria should be used for defining the degree of dechristianization in "a secular age"? Does not secularization mean rather a quest for new religious forms (when the older ones do not suffice) – so a sort of dechristianization and rechristianization at the same time?[33] Trutz Rendtorff sees the counter-productivity of usual theological diagnoses of modern times in two respects: (i) in an implicit but normative fixation of what should be considered to be "Christian" or

---

[28] The title of one of Barth's books *Enlightened Protestantism* (*Aufgeklärter Protestantismus* [Tübingen: Mohr Siebeck, 2004]) says volumes.

[29] Cf. Lauster, *Religion als Lebensdeutung*, pp. 147-152.

[30] Friedrich Gogarten, *Verhängnis und Hoffnung der Neuzeit. Die Säkularisierung als theologisches Problem* (Stuttgart: Siebenstern, ²1958), p. 99.

[31] Gogarten, *Verhängnis und Hoffnung der Neuzeit*, 94-95. In addition, Barth refers to Romano Guardini, Hans Küng, Helmut Thielicke, Carl Heinz Ratschow and particularly Wolfhart Pannenberg who adopt the structural connection between secularization and the Enlightenment. While the earlier Pannenberg finds "the Christian legitimacy of the modern times" (Pannenberg, *Gottesgedanke und menschliche Freiheit*, p. 128), the later Pannenberg says: "Modern secularism... is itself a by-product [orig. *Verfallsprodukt*] of the cultural tradition so strongly shaped by Christianity". Wolfhart Pannenberg, *Systematic Theology* II, translated by Geoffrey W. Bromiley (London/New York: T&T Clark, 2004), p. xii.

[32] Barth, "Säkularisierung und Moderne," p. 138.

[33] Cf. Hartmut Lehmann, *Säkularisierung, Dechristianisierung, Rechristianisierung im neuzeitlichen Europa* (Göttingen: Vandenhoeck & Ruprecht, 1997).

"religious" and (ii) in an effort to find an excuse for our own failures in presenting the contents of Christian tradition.[34]

The complexities of the history of ideas makes it impossible to just accuse European Enlightenment of anti-religious tendencies or of hostility towards Christianity. The various contributions of the Enlightenment to the religious condition of modernity have to be judged much more carefully than just by using the pejorative term "secularism".[35] In fact the diverse impulses of the Enlightenment extended to the entire cultural sphere and they stemmed from various different motives. Generally, it was "a cultural-historical reaction to the big crises of the confessional age".[36] The Enlightenment struggle against traditional creeds, institutionalized dogmas and obsolete beliefs created space for – despite occasional waves of militant atheism – "more flexible, subjectively more comprehensible options of piety."[37] Criticism and defence of religion often go hand in hand and they are argumentatively interconnected in Enlightenment thought. The Enlightenment thinkers look for a non-dogmatic understanding of religion and a non-confessional conception of Christianity. Moreover, the Enlightenment understood itself in an important sense as the *religious* enlightenment as Emanuel Hirsch pointed out. "Only in religion – where it is about relation of an unconditional certainty to an unconditional content – human reason could catch sight of its own strength and thus limit itself."[38] If the beliefs of the past have stood this "litmus test" they in fact gained in their plausibility. The Enlightenment has protected religion from its fundamentalist forms. Reasonability in faith, revelation and Christianity – that has been the main purpose of the Enlightenment criticism of religion. The Enlightenment is not a product of arbitrary moods but an outcome of serious *seeking* – not simply "the result"[39] of – rationally acceptable answers to a long and broad stream of

---

[34] Cf. Trutz Rendtorff, "Säkularisierung als theologisches Problem", *NZSTh*, 4 (1962), pp. 318-339; Martin Laube, *Theologie und neuzeitliches Christentum* (Tübingen: Mohr Siebeck, 2006), pp. 221-229.

[35] This term appeared most likely for the first time in the "Leicester Secular Society", founded by George J. Holyoake in 1851, to denote its liberal-humanistic program. The term "secularism" referred to the secular space as the only appropriate space for welfare efforts under the conditions of the modern pluralistic society. But the aggressive anti-religious contours of the program of Holyoake's successors have shifted the meaning of this term to imply a crypto-religious promise of an intra-worldly salvation. Cf. Barth, p. 143.

[36] Lauster, *Religion als Lebensdeutung*, p. 149.

[37] Barth, "Säkularisierung und Moderne," p. 139.

[38] Barth, "Säkularisierung und Moderne," p. 139.

[39] So Barth, "Säkularisierung und Moderne," p. 140.

issues and questions whose urgency increases if we close our eyes to them. There is, thank God, no return to Christianity before the Enlightenment. Being aware of the real motives behind Enlightenment we can understand better the problems of modernity which in fact go far beyond the Enlightenment as a historical movement.[40] First of all the problem of secularization.

SECULARIZATION AS A HERMENEUTICAL CATEGORY OF THE CRISIS OF RELIGION

Critical factors of modernization

The early Friedrich Schleiermacher in his *Speeches* (1799) pointed out that the religious critique of the Enlightenment has to be understood on a deeper level than was usually the case. It was not the militant atheists but rather the too practically oriented people inside and outside religious communities who have been the real gravediggers of religion! The way they insisted on a clear explanation of everything and practical usefulness in *all* areas of life raised the finite human mind to the status of definitive measure of all interpretations of reality. Within the framework of functional logic of modern social systems the perspectives of wholeness, transcendence and infiniteness, which are absolutely essential for religion, wane and disappear. At the same time, the empiricist and utilitarian reductionism has developed enormously and penetrated all areas of the contemporary understanding of reality. It is true that "modernity opens up new perspectives for both the domain of secularity and the domain of religiosity by drawing due distinctions between the finite and the infinite, between the transcendent and the immanent sense of action."[41] But there is an absolute lack of social preconditions for the subjective relevance of belief in modern – secularized – societies.[42] In order to clarify the structural aggravation of the situation, Ulrich Barth, employing a sociological perspective, presents the following characteristics of modernity: bureaucracy, capitalism, technology, democratization and information media.[43] I add

---

[40] Cf. Barth, "Säkularisierung und Moderne," p. 140.

[41] Dierken, *Selbstbewußtsein individueller Freiheit*, pp. 57-58.

[42] Cf. Alois Hahn, *Religion und der Verlust der Sinngebung. Identitäts probleme in der modernen Gesellschaft* (Frankfurt a. M.: Herder, 1974), p. 116.

[43] Cf. Barth, pp. 146-156. Jörg Dierken mentions five more phenomena: disciplining, industrialization, scientification, objectification and disenchantment. Cf. Dierken, *Selbstbewußtsein individueller Freiheit*, 55.

one more characteristic which may be viewed as a consequence of those five: loss of gratitude.

Bureaucracy. The differentiation of social roles is one of the very bases of human coexistence. It is biologically anchored in gender identities and generational difference and it is strengthened culturally and conventionally. The more complex a given society is, the more it distinguishes particular social roles. The social system responds to it similarly: in the society as a whole, a maximum performance is achieved with minimum effort only if the different subsystems work individually but cooperatively. The interactions between the functional areas and their inter-dependence have to be clearly defined for all of them. The complex structure of social subsystems is called bureaucracy. This term applies not only to an apparatus of public administration. Bureaucracy has far-reaching anthropological consequences: a process analogical to the structural differentiation of society is going on in human mind in which – as inter alia Dilthey and Simmel say – more individuals intersect. The subject, being obliged to play various different roles, is increasingly alienated from her or his true self – in this heteronomy lies the profoundest of all the "crises of subjectivity".[44] It is here where we have to look for the causes of the rapid development towards individualization and privatization in modernity. The high degree of bureaucratic structures at *all* levels of social and individual life is a result of rationalisation processes which aim to satisfy the urgent need for effectiveness.[45] Culture has become a limited sector of society – and the so called theologians of the Word of God have even taught: whereas culture is over there, Christian religion is here.[46]

The contemporary degree of bureaucracy is precarious for social and individual functions of religion. Religious consciousness grasps and encompasses the whole area of human existence as the traditional concepts of Christian anthropology show. There is no being a creature, no sin and no need of salvation without God's total determination of human being in her or his religious self-consciousness. But a particular

---

[44] Cf. Ingolf U. Dalferth and Philipp Stoellger (eds.), *Krisen der Subjektivität: Problem feldereinesstrittigen Paradigmas* (Tübingen: Mohr Siebeck, 2005).

[45] Cf. Barth, "Säkularisierung und Moderne," pp. 146-147.

[46] Cf. Ulrich H. J. Körtner, *Theologie des Wortes Gottes: Positionen – Probleme – Perspektiven* (Göttingen: Vandenhoeck & Ruprecht, 2001), p. 26: Against a supposed "crisis of culture", the theology of the Word of God has claimed "an insurmountable contradiction, the diastase, the qualitative distance between Christianity and culture, between God and human being."

individual perceives religion as one of her or his roles. In addition to religion, there are many other roles with their particular perspectives. The segmentation of social areas leads ultimately to the fragmentation of one's identity awareness. Religion coexists in plurality – not to say in competition – with other lifestyle options and so it expresses only a sub-identity of the modern human being. The real problem of modern pluralism is contingency which retroactively reinforces pluralism.[47] Of course, there are many reasons to take pluralism as a value and a chance.[48] However, the constant increase of the number of choices and decisions may be experienced not as a realization of one's freedom but as an "overstraining compulsion to be free."[49] Under these conditions, religion cannot set norms for the spectrum of roles but thanks to its unifying nature, it could provide a transcending ground for one's multiple sub-identities. There is a strong need for such unity, as the success of "wandering religiosity" (Ernst Troeltsch)[50] and various "pseudo-religious" or "surrogate religious"[51] movements with their cults of personality show. Nonetheless, the stabilizing effect of religion may be reached only through inhabiting a particular culture of self-interpretation.[52]

Capitalism. The inner-worldly pursuit of happiness and success in life corresponds with analogous religious motives and follows their strategies in dealing with the risk of contingency with which success is

---

[47] Cf. the historical, sociological and psychological objections of Hans Joas to Peter L. Berger's conception of pluralism: *Braucht der Mensch Religion?*, pp. 32-49.

[48] Cf. Joas, *Braucht der Mensch Religion?*, p. 37: "...a flexible internalisation of norms and values" may lead to an "intensified attention to the other in myself and beyond myself" as well as to "overcoming of the compulsiveness towards a similarly dynamic (instead of static) stability as the discourse achieves it at institutional level."

[49] Joas, *Braucht der Mensch Religion?*, p. 32.

[50] Cf. Friedrich Wilhelm Graf, *Die Wiederkehr der Götter. Religion in der modernen Kultur* (Munich: Beck, 2004), p. 96.

[51] I use this term for lack of conceptual instruments. Cf. Hartmut Lehmann, *Protestantisches Christentum im Prozeß der Säkularisierung* (Göttingen: Vandenhoeck & Ruprecht, 2001), p. 32: "If in view of the redemption potential of the big ideologies of the 20th century we still use terms such as 'pseudo'-religions or 'surrogate' religions, it becomes obvious how little we have succeeded in developing a convincing terminology for the description of the religious power of these phenomena."

[52] Cf. Barth, "Säkularisierung und Moderne," pp. 148-149.

always connected.[53] Increasing efficiency and maximalizing profit are the essential motivation factors for economic behaviour – by no means only since the beginning of modernity. But only since the invention of market economy have they become the ultimate criterion. The very substance of modern capitalism lies in mutual reinforcement of the increase in profit motivation and profitability calculation. The success of the capitalist system reveals its downside, namely the tendency to subordinate all non-economic mechanisms to its own system logic. Many varieties of the price/performance thinking, cost/benefit evaluation, cost/income calculation determine not only almost all areas of everyday interaction but penetrate into emotional and mental constellations and the world of subjective experience.[54] The rhetoric of *homo debitor*, a kitschy form of secularized hamartiology with an almost religious pathos, dominates the public space; all social spheres are infected with the imperative of "repaying debts", which actually disguises the real and more urgent debts – primarily the debt of the ecological trace, in the Czech Republic one of the deepest in Europe.[55] "Inquisitors of the blinded monotheism of economic growth" exclude all voices calling for a 'non-growth economy' from the public space".[56] The "fundamentalist religion of the growth of Growth, which has its temples – supermarkets, and its high priests – managers and brokers, its rituals and languages – advertising and manager ptydepe,"[57] joins dominant right- and left-wing parties to "a big growth party".[58] With the exception of "the fetish of economic growth", "modern societies offer no shared meaning". "But if it would break down, it would in fact endanger also the necessary social cohesion."[59] Europe lives in the times of "a post-democratic capitalism", it means in a system "without any outside" – all its "alternatives" have become part of it.[60] Our capitalism is more and

---

[53] Cf. Dierken, *Fortschritte in der Geschichte der Religion?*, p. 229.

[54] Cf. Barth, "Säkularisierung und Moderne," p. 150.

[55] Cf. Václav Bělohradský, *Mezi světy & mezisvěty. Reloaded 2013* (Prague: Novela bohemica, 2013), p. 19.

[56] Bělohradský, *Mezi světy & mezisvěty*, p. 20.

[57] Václav Bělohradský, *Společnost nevolnosti. Eseje z pozdější doby* (Prague: SLON, ³2014), p. 9. "Ptydepe" is an artificial language from the play *The Memorandum* (1965) by Václav Havel.

[58] Bělohradský, *Mezi světy & mezisvěty*, p. 20.

[59] Jan Sokol, "Politika, náboženství a veřejný prostor," online: http://www.jansokol.cz/2014/03/politika-nabozenstvi-a-verejny-prostor/[August 21, 2014].

[60] Cf. Bělohradský, *Mezi světy & mezisvěty*, p. 24.

Democracy. The process of establishing political democracy, initiated through the French Revolution, has not remained limited to the political sphere only but has influenced other areas of public life as well. This process in fact soon also affected institutionalized Christianity. Some Protestant denominations partly – and without much enthusiasm – implemented democratic principles and mechanisms in their inner structure. Church leaders gradually became accountable not only to Church synods but also to the ordinary Church members. Critical feedback from Church members communicated to Church leaders has become a new dynamic factor as it applied not only to individual cases within the ecclesial institution but also to the institution as such. Church membership does not really imply confessional belonging any more. *Christianity outside the Church*[71] becomes more and more widespread. The traditional theologically defined distinction between clergy and lay people grows weaker (see for example the lay ecclesial movement "We Are Church" in Germany). All these trends show that the general democratizing processes and the egalitarian tendencies to let all those who wish to participate in decision making codetermine whatever happens influence the transformations of religious life as well.[72]

Media. All forms of symbolic communication depend on media which also determine the degree of their publicity. The deepest transformation in the development of public communication up to now has been the introduction of mass media. The relation between the use of mass media on the one hand and the origin and function of public opinion on the other hand has become an independent theme in sociological research. The new quality of communication and the acceleration of the speed of data transmission require an inner criterion for "newsworthiness". It is called "information" – not in the sense of information theory but in the sense of novelty of content. One can hardly distinguish between *factum* and *fictum* in the public space because media are "self-inflammatory", to use the expression of Václav Havel.[73] The attractiveness of consumed information is not measured by the strength of the impulses but rather by their "surprise value". "The information tempo becomes an independent experiential content."[74]

The sphere of religion is affected by these changes to a high degree, especially in the very form of its public expression – in the cult.

---

[71] Cf. Trutz Rendtorff, *Christentum außerhalb der Kirche: Konkretionen der Aufklärung* (Hamburg: Furche, 1969).

[72] Cf. Barth, "Säkularisierung und Moderne," pp. 153-154.

[73] Cf. Bělohradský, *Společnost nevolnosti*, pp. 10.313-321.

[74] Barth, "Säkularisierung und Moderne," p. 154-155; here p.155.

Religious communication originates (anthropologically speaking) in cultic-ritual performance which in archaic times consisted primarily of sacrificial rites. An important landmark in the development of religious communication came with the rise of – to use a too schematic and imprecise term – "book religions". These religions have transferred the core of religious communication to the recitation and exegesis of sacred texts. Protestantism presupposes this situation and gives it probably the most stringent expression within Christianity. That is why Protestantism is particularly affected by the consequences of the epochal transformation process of the modern communication.[75]

The culture of religious interpretation tends to be exclusivist. Therefore, it has always stood in confrontation with alternative forms of social and individual search for meaning which are flourishing in the situation of pluralism. Besides substantive oppositions there is an ongoing competition in the area of media presentation of the alternative options. Traditional forms of religious communication have to prove themselves in the face of modern worlds of experience. The dynamics of media communication are contrary to almost all the essential elements of traditional modes of religious presentation. On the one hand, being flooded by a rapid sequence of diverse attractive impressions, presenting real life situations and experiences, anonymity of media consumption, and characteristic slowness and monotony of rites, abstractness of high-level religious symbols which are therefore quite distant from everyday experience and the typically religious obligation to take a stance etc. on the other hand. Yet if some form of religious communication aims at overcoming this structural contrast by trying to fascinate, it will lead to a creeping loss of its formative power, and even to a decline of its interest in participating in the official cult. "In highly developed information societies, this state of affairs has been reached."[76]

Loss of gratitude. "And what hast thou that thou didst not receive?"[77] Religious interpretation of reality is a grateful one. "The feeling of absolute dependence" and "the feeling of absolute gratitude" are two sides of the same coin. One experiences her or his life as an undeserved gift. Each morning or even each moment is a feast. The religious attitude to life does not know any "profanity"; everything is "sacred". The religious believer perceives a "dimension" of Sacredness, Absoluteness, Infinity and the Unconditional in all life-world constellations. Worship is a response to the feeling of absolute gratitude

---

[75] Cf. Barth, "Säkularisierung und Moderne," p. 155.
[76] Barth, "Säkularisierung und Moderne," pp. 155-156; here p. 156.
[77] 1K 4:7 (KJV).

which it deepens. In spite of all the developed welfare system, all modern individualized societies emphasize the ability to be independent and to help oneself in the case of danger. The religious attitude therefore seems more and more redundant and gratitude is felt only in extraordinary situations, maybe after one survives a disaster. Yet, the most important things in our life we cannot buy but only get for free: health, happiness, a harmonious family and good friends; it is that way in modern societies as well.[78] In consequence of the above described secularization factors, this awareness seems to be fading – as well as the awareness of being an heir of common spiritual values. People rather tend to think: *I am entitled to be healthy because I pay the health insurance myself. I am entitled to enjoy good weather because my vacation was not cheap.* The loss of gratitude, as a result of taking everything for granted and assuming disponibility of one's own life and its contents, has far-reaching hamartiological implications. The modern human being is not troubled with her or his sin. The general self-reliance strengthens the need for self-justification. Self-justification, however, is no more than self-delusion. Of course, if the religious attitude is not natural anymore, religion "may be deeper, heartier, truer and freer."[79] It can "protect one from the feeling of uselessness and boredom" as well as "open eyes for the needs of others, for the beauty of bravery, purity, modesty and selfless service and so offer the ultimate meaning to the human freedom."[80] But without the feeling of gratitude there is no experience of justification – and no religion.

CONCLUSION

Under the conditions of modernity, the difficulties of religious consciousness to realize and "project" itself have increased greatly. The dynamic effects of our times upon religious consciousness prove to be specifically modern phenomena. We are living on the ruins of modernity, as the postmodernity discourse reminds us. Europe experiences neither the end of Christianity, nor a change of religious forms but a turbulent transformation of the social and individual self-consciousness. It is characterized by a feeling of an "identitarian panic", as the Czech philosopher Václav Bělohradský expresses it concisely.

---

[78] Cf. Sokol, "Civilizace, kultura, náboženství," p. 224 and Jan Sokol, "Politika, náboženství a veřejný prostor," available online, see: http://www.jansokol.cz/2014/03/politika-nabozenstvi-a-verejny-prostor/ [August 21, 2014].
[79] Sokol, "Civilizace, kultura, náboženství," p. 224.
[80] Sokol, "Civilizace, kultura, náboženství," p. 226.

The dictum of Georg Simmel remains true, even though it was said more than a century ago: "[O]ur age..., on the whole, certainly possesses more freedom than any previous one [but it] is unable to enjoy it properly."[81] The declining public space, paralyzed by strategic mystifications, becomes less and less productive. It is ruled by "an unholy alliance of the entertainment industry, *identitarian* aggression and consumerism."[82] We experience a big turn from an identity based on argumentation to an argumentation based on identity.[83] In fact, the power of articulating Christian convictions in secular language and its cultivation are from a long-term perspective hardly thinkable without Churches.[84] They often represent more a *celebritas Dei* than the *Gloria Dei*.[85] I do not dare to estimate how the existing Churches will cope with this situation and what role they will play. But I firmly hope that this question will have the potential of being interesting not only for believers and theologians.

BIBLIOGRAPHY

Barth, Ulrich. 2003. "Säkularisierung und Moderne. Die soziokulturelle Transformation der Religion." In *Religion in der Moderne*. Tübingen: Mohr Siebeck, 2003, 127-165.
Barth, Ulrich. 2004. *Aufgeklärter Protestantismus*. Tübingen: Mohr Siebeck.
Bělohradský, Václav. 2013. *Mezi světy & mezisvěty. Reloaded 2013*. Prague: Novela bohemica.
Bělohradský, Václav. 2014. *Společnost nevolnosti. Eseje z pozdější doby*. Prague: SLON.
Dalferth, Ingolf U. and Stoellger, Philipp (eds.). 2005. *Krisen der Subjektivität: Problem feldereinesstrittigen Paradigmas*. Tübingen: Mohr Siebeck.

---

[81] Georg Simmel, *The Philosophy of Money*, David Frisby (ed.) (London/New York: Routledge, 2005 [1910]), p. 406. I am grateful to Prof. Dr. Jan Sokol for the reference of this quote.

[82] Bělohradský, *Mezi světy & mezisvěty*, p. 16.

[83] In the Czech Protestant milieu, an anthology arose called *Searching: Studies and Essays on the Protestant Identity* (Ondřej Macek [ed.], *Zpytování: Studie a eseje k evangelické identitě* [Středokluky: Zdeněk Susa, 2007]).

[84] Cf. Dierken, *Selbstbewußtsein individueller Freiheit*, p. 53.

[85] Cf. Václav Bělohradský, "Od gloria (dei) k celebritas (dei). Papežovy smažené bramborůrky žádejte v snack-barech Sabritas!," in *Společnost nevolnosti*, pp. 77-84.

Dierken, Jörg. 2005. *Selbstbewußtsein individueller Freiheit. Religionstheoretische Erkundungen in protestantischer Perspektive.* Tübingen: Mohr Siebeck.
Dierken, Jörg. 2012. *Fortschritte in der Geschichte der Religion? Aneignungeiner Denkfigur der Aufklärung*, ThLZ.F 24. Leipzig: Evangelische Verlagsanstalt.
Frühwald, Wolfgang. 2001. "Der optimierte Mensch." *Forschung & Lehre*. No. 8, 402-405.
Gogarten, Friedrich. 1958. *Verhängnis und Hoffnung der Neuzeit. Die Säkularisierung als theologisches Problem*. Stuttgart: Siebenstern.
Graf, Friedrich Wilhelm. 2004. *Die Wiederkehr der Götter. Religion in der modernen Kultur*. Munich: Beck.
Habermas, Jürgen. 2001. *Glauben und Wissen*. Frankfurt a. M.: Buchhändler-Vereinigung.
Hahn, Alois. 1974. *Religion und der Verlust der Sinngebung. Identitäts probleme in der modernen Gesellschaft*. Frankfurt a. M.: Herder.
Hejdánek, Ladislav. "Ještě křesťanství a náboženství" (1966). In *Filosofie a víra. Nepředmětnost v myšlení a ve skutečnosti* II. Prague: OIKOYMENH, 53-56.
Hejdánek, Ladislav. 1999. "Víra v sekularizovaném světě" (1962). In *Filosofie a víra. Nepředmětnost v myšlení a ve skutečnosti* II. Prague: OIKOYMENH, 26-34.
Hejdánek, Ladislav. 2012. *Úvod do filosofování*. Part 4 (1971). Prague: OIKOYMENH, 64-78.
Hošek, Pavel. 2008. "Prolegomena k interdisciplinárnímu tázání po vztahu evropské sekularity a západního křesťanství," *Sociální studia*. No. 3-4, 15-26.
Hromádka, Josef L. 1958. *Evangelium o cestě za člověkem. Úvod do studia Písem a církevních vyznání*. Prague: Kalich.
Joas, Hans. 2004. *Braucht der Mensch Religion? Über Erfahrungen der Selbsttranszendenz*. Freiburg/Basel/Wien: Herder.
Joas, Hans. 2012. *Glaube als Option. Zukunftsmöglichkeiten des Christentums*. Freiburg: Herder.
Körtner, Ulrich H. J. 2001. *Theologie des Wortes Gottes: Positionen – Probleme – Perspektiven*. Göttingen: Vandenhoeck & Ruprecht.
Laube, Martin. 2006. *Theologie und neuzeitliches Christentum*. Tübingen: Mohr Siebeck.
Lauster, Jörg. 2005. *Religion als Lebensdeutung: Theologische Hermeneutik heute*. Darmstadt: Wissenschaftliche Buchgesellschaft.
Lehmann, Hartmut. 2001. *Protestantisches Christentum im Prozeß der Säkularisierung*. Göttingen: Vandenhoeck & Ruprecht.
Lehmann, Hartmut. 2009. "Ein europäischer Sonderweg in Sachen Religion." in *Europäische Religionsgeschichte. Ein mehrfacher*

Pluralismus I, Kippenberg, Hans G., Rüpke, Jörg and Stuckrad, Kocku von (eds.). Göttingen: Vandenhoeck & Ruprecht.
Lehmann, Hartmut. 1997. *Säkularisierung, Dechristianisierung, Rechristianisierung im neuzeitlichen Europa*. Göttingen: Vandenhoeck & Ruprecht.
Lübbe, Hartmut. 1965. *Säkularisierung. Geschichte eines ideenpolitischen Begriffs*. Freiburg/München: Alber.
Luckmann, Thomas. 1991. "The New and the Old in Religion." in Bourdieu, Pierre and Coleman, James S. (eds.). *Social Theory for a Changing Society*. Boulder/San Francisco/Oxford: Westview, 167-188.
Macek, Ondřej (ed.). 2007. *Zpytování: Studie a eseje k evangelické identitě*. Středokluky: Zdeněk Susa.
Pannenberg, Wolfhart. 1972. *Gottesgedanke und menschliche Freiheit*. Göttingen: Vandenhoeck & Ruprecht.
Pannenberg, Wolfhart. 1983. *Anthropologie in theologischer Perspektive*. Göttingen: Vandenhoeck & Ruprecht.
Pannenberg, Wolfhart. 2004. *Systematic Theology* II, translated by Geoffrey W. Bromiley. London/New York: T&T Clark.
Rendtorff, Trutz. 1962. "Säkularisierung als theologisches Problem", *Neue Zeitschrift für Systematische Theologie und Religionsphilosophie*, Vol. 4. No. 2, 318-339.
Rendtorff, Trutz. 1969. *Christentum außerhalb der Kirche: Konkretionen der Aufklärung*. Hamburg: Furche.
Schleiermacher, Friedrich D. E. 1984 [1799]. *Über die Religion. Reden and die Gebildeten unter ihren Verächtern*. In *Kritische Gesamtausgabe* I/2: *Schriften aus der Berliner Zeit 1769-1799*, Meckenstock, Günter (ed.). Berlin: Walter de Gruyter.
Simmel, Georg. 2005 [1910]. *The Philosophy of Money*. Frisby, David (ed.). London/New York: Routledge.
Smolík, Josef. 1973. "Poznámky k elaborátu J. Ellula." *Křesťanská revue*. Vol. 40, 93.
Sokol, Jan. "Politika, náboženství a veřejný prostor." online: http://www.jansokol.cz/2014/03/politika-nabozenstvi-a-verejny-prostor/[August 21, 2014].
Sokol, Jan. 1999. "Politika a náboženství." in *Demokracie a ústavnost*, Kunc, Jan (ed.). Prague: Karolinum, 232-237.
Sokol, Jan. 2010. *Malá filosofie člověka a Slovník současných pojmů*. Prague: Vyšehrad.
Sprondel, Gottfried. 1985. "Die Legende vom 'religionslosen Zeitalter'. Auch in der nachchristlichen Wirklichkeit wird nach Gott gefragt." *Lutherische Monatshefte*. Vol. 24. No. 12, 557-561.

CHAPTER V

A POSTMODERN QUEST: SEEKING GOD AND RELIGIOUS LANGUAGE IN A POSTMODERN CONTEXT

MARTIN KOČÍ

The theme of seeking God in a postmodern context reminds me about an experience which Tomáš Halík describes in his book *Patience with God*. Once, Halík saw on the wall of a subway station the inscription "Jesus is the answer!" Everyone finds such words on the walls all over the world from time to time. This inscription, however, was not like the others. Someone else had added the following words: "But what was the question?"[1] This humorous scene, in my opinion, reveals something important, something that we may easily forget. In short, when we dare to speak about God, questions are far more important than answers.

The Church experiences difficulties in finding a new phase in the relationship to the world she wants to speak with. Charles Taylor clearly points out that the phenomenon of seekers, and not only the phenomenon but their very presence, is rather neglected.

There is a mode of spiritual seeking which is very widespread in the West today, but which the official Church often seems to want to rebuff. Seekers ask questions, but the official Church seems largely concerned with pushing certain already worked-out answers. It seems to have little capacity to listen.[2]

Who are these seekers? According to Taylor, they are people looking for authenticity. They expect the Church to create a place of authenticity instead of a place of power. I dare to add another distinctive element. Seekers live in the midst of an uncertain postmodern world; a world which is full of challenges, doubts, and questions. In short, seekers are the *people of questions*. What method should be applied in

---

[1] Cf. Tomáš Halík, *Patience with God: The Story of Zacchaeus Continuing in Us* (New York: Doubleday, 2009), p. 6.

[2] Quoted from George F. McLean, "Disjunctions in the 21st Century," in: *Church and People: Disjunctions in a Secular Age*, ed. Ch. Taylor, J. Casanova and G. F. McLean (Washington: Council for Research in Values & Philosophy, 2012), p. 5.

order to approach them? What language should be used to address them? These questions summarize the main task of this chapter.

A DOUBLE CHALLENGE

The Church faces a double challenge in a secular postmodern context. The difficulty of communicating faith applies both *ad extra* (in the public square) as well as *ad intra* (in the Church). In both cases we are confronted with the problem of language. How to talk about God in a new understandable way? How to appeal to seekers without being coercive? And, last but not least, to whom does the Church want to speak?

Perhaps the language problems of the Church are caused by the wrong reading of the current situation through the so-called secular paradigm. It presupposes an old-fashioned bipolar distinction between believers and non-believers; the Christian Church and the secular world.[3] Not to mention that this bi-polar reading, suggesting an ongoing fight between the secular and the religious, is tempting the Church to build up a ghetto and consequently neglect real problems and challenges. Through this prism, theology can rather easily distinguish between two groups of people: believers and non-believers, and perhaps add another group of those who are somewhere *in between*, sometimes closer to the religious position, and at other times closer to the non-religious position. This analysis naturally influences the way of theologizing and consequently, the manner of communicating the Christian message. It informs the method in which the Church addresses believers, conducts dialogue with non-believers and, last but not least, appeals to the grey-zone in between. But what if the grey zone were not that grey? It is difficult though to set off on a journey into unknown water and leave the secure place of the secular paradigm behind.

The claim that the secular paradigm is a wrong reading of the current times and, thus, all the attempts to solve the problem, based on this wrong interpretation, are doomed,[4] does not suggest that the Western context is not secular in terms of Taylor's opus magnum, *A Secular Age*. Without any doubts (1) God/religion has been removed from the public square (politics, social questions, public policy, etc.); (2) the number of Church goers is continually decreasing; (3) the conditions

---

[3] Cf. Martin Kočí, "Jeden ze ztracených klíčů," *Universum* 20, no. 2 (2010): pp. 38-40.

[4] For example, the project of New Evangelization fails to recognize new shifts in the current context which cannot be described as simply secular.

of belief have changed.[5] The Church acknowledges the first point, deals with the second point, but nevertheless almost neglects the third point. Nonetheless, it is *secularization 3* that is the most interesting, for Taylor as well as for us. If we want to understand seekers (meaning: who they are? and what they seek?), we must be courageous and admit that the conditions of Christian belief have changed. We must recognize that to be placed *in between* believers and non-believers today means something substantially different from only a few decades ago.

It seems more reasonable and adequate to describe our context in terms of detraditionalisation and pluralisation.[6] What does it mean? Detraditionalisation implies that traditions and identities (religious, secular, political, etc.) do not pass from one generation to another. An individual identity is not pre-given any more. Neither Christianity, nor any other basic story is able to grant an unquestionable and secure identity in a postmodern context. This opinion is based on Jean-François Lyotard and his claim that postmodern conditions can be defined "as incredulity towards metanarratives."[7] Even though some theologians do not subscribe to this diagnosis fully, they mostly agree that the problem of communicating faith is linked to the identity problem.[8] Identity must be constructed in the interaction with pluralistic context. Pluralisation describes the richness and colourfulness of the contemporary era as well as an endless opportunity to choose. On the one hand, the Church faces an ongoing decontextualization of individual identities. On the other hand, individual identities must be more reflexive and open. In sum, the Church, in its commendable effort to approach people beyond its own borders, must be aware that there is no common Christian background. Perhaps there is no common background at all.[9]

---

[5] Cf. Charles Taylor, *A Secular Age* (Cambridge, MT: Harvard University Press, 2007), pp. 1-25.

[6] Cf. Lieven Boeve, *God Interrupts History: Theology in a Time of Upheaval* (New York: Continuum, 2007), pp. 16–26.

[7] Jean François Lyotard, *The Postmodern Condition: A Report on Knowledge* (Minneapolis: University of Minnesota Press, 1984), p. xxiv.

[8] For example, Nicholas Lash does not agree with Lyotard's accusation that all grand narratives lapse necessarily into hegemonic patterns. "The Christian story of everything, I have been suggesting, is the story of God's being as gift, as self-gift establishing and enlivening the world." According to Lash, although Christians participate in a grand narrative, they have to bear in mind its givenness. The Christian narrative is, therefore, not in the possession of Christians but something received from the Giver of everything. Nicholas Lash, *Holiness, Speech and Silence: Reflections on the Question of God* (Aldershot, Burlington, VT: Ashgate Pub., 2004), pp. 23–49; quotation: p. 43.

[9] Cf. Boeve, *God Interrupts History*, p. 51.

Assuming the current context of Christianity, it would not be a surprise that there is a certain difficulty of communicating faith *ad extra*.

The Christian experience of reality can only be adequately communicated to those who have a minimal familiarity with the particularities of the Christian narrative, or are at least prepared to become acquainted with it.... The Christian narrative constitutes its own (dynamic) symbolic space, that is, its own hermeneutical horizon. Becoming acquainted with Christianity is thus something akin to learning a language, a complex event that presumes grammar, vocabulary, formation of habits, and competence as much as it does empathy.... This implies as well that if one wants to know something of Christianity, one will have to familiarize oneself to a certain degree with its narratives, vocabulary, practices, and views – regardless of whether one is sharing (or is willing to share) them or not.[10]

From the opposite side, the omnipresent temptation to petrify historical forms of Christian narrative implies difficulties with regard to communicating faith *ad intra*. "The contextual changes put pressure on the Christian tradition as it has been given shape in the previous decades and centuries and is handed down to us."[11] Charles Taylor refers to the same problem in his essay "The Church Speaks – To Whom?" Seekers have a feeling "that the answers given by the Churches are just too quick, too pat, that they do not reflect a search."[12]

In sum, we deal with the double language problem. On the one hand, the Church has trouble with an old language no longer understandable among the dwellers. On the other hand, it is barely possible to communicate even the Christian basics in a context which is not familiar with the symbolic language of Christianity.

Outsiders need to familiarize themselves with the 'narrative thickness' of Christianity in order to understand it. Insiders need to bear witness to *Deus semper maior* in their God-talk. However, it is a mistake to mix up these two different problems of language. "The ad intra problem of searching for a new language is often wrongly seen as the

---

[10] Lieven Boeve, "Communicating Faith in Contemporary Europe: Dealing with Language Problems in and outside the Church," in *Communicating Faith*, ed. John Sullivan (Washington, D.C: Catholic University of America Press, 2011), pp. 302–303.

[11] Ibid., p. 303.

[12] Charles Taylor, "The Church Speak – To Whom?," in *Church and People: Disjunctions in a Secular Age*, ed. Charles Taylor, José Casanova and George F. McLean, Cultural heritage and contemporary change. Series 8. Christian philosophical studies 1 (Washington, D.C.: Council for Research in Values and Philosophy, 2012), p. 18.

solution for the communication problems ad extra."[13] In other words, the internal renewal – a new theological language – does not solve the problem. And vice versa, the recuperation of cultural standards – changing theological language – does not make the Christian narrative more authentic.

We find ourselves in a peculiar situation. We must search for a theologically legitimate and contextually plausible language. We can never speak about God adequately, but we must do it. Who could help us? What about postmodern philosophy and postmodern thinkers? Indeed, it seems that postmodern authors in their so-called 'turn to religion' might be of help. Moreover, the theme of language is for them crucial. Perhaps we will find some inspiration there.

POSTMODERN IMPULSES

Postmodern philosophers try to avoid the trap of language because they rightly fear the temptation to exhaust mystery in inappropriate words. The spectre of onto-theology portraying God in schematic definitions is still haunting around as an undesirable heritage of modernity.[14] Thus, postmodern authors often begin to think about the problem of naming God from the following presupposition:

> Our religious language tries to bring God under control, to assimilate God within our ready-made systems of meaning, to turn God into a reassuring projection of our own need and desires. Such religious language is a barrier against God's strangeness: that is why God's attack on language is launched primarily against the beachhead of human religiosity.[15]

---

[13] Lieven Boeve, "Communicating Faith in Contemporary Europe, p. 305. Boeve expressed the same even before: "It would be a misconception, however, to think that recontextualization is capable of solving the entire communication problem, let alone that it has the capacity to convince non-Christians, ex-Christians (or even potential Christians) once again of the validity of the Christian narrative. The ad extra problem is not in the first place a matter of the renewal of faith language, but of the familiarity with it (initiation)." Boeve, *God Interrupts History*, p. 54.

[14] I elaborate on this problem in Martin Kočí, "God in Question: Questioning as a Prerequisite for Theology," *Acta Universitatis Carolinae Theologica* 4, no. 1 (2014): pp. 51-66.

[15] Benjamin Myers, *Christ the Stranger: The Theology of Rowan Williams* (London, New York: T&T Clark, 2012), pp. 32–33.

Jean-Luc Marion, for example, suggests a radical phenomenological approach to naming God.[16] In line with classical phenomenology, Marion considers a human subject to be a passive recipient of what appears to him/her. For Marion, however, what appears is given and, thus, "the whole metaphysics of *naming* God must give way to a new understanding of God as pure *giving*."[17] Religious language is only responsive to this primal givenness. Thus, for Marion, there is a pre-linguistic universal structure of religion. This structure presupposes an absolutely passive subject in a totally asymmetrical relationship with the other-God. At the end of the day, Marion ends up in a purely negative theology without any intention to name God. "It is not what is being said that is of real importance, but that something is said."[18] By doing so, Marion tries to overcome the onto-theological paradigm. Paradoxically, he creates a new onto-theological structure of an absolute impossibility to name God. One is simply lost in the darkness of negations. Theologians must ask: does the refusal to name the other (God) serve us better?

Jacques Derrida and John D. Caputo propose a radical hermeneutical approach to religion based on the philosophy of deconstruction. They suggest the concept of 'pure religion' without/beyond religion.[19] For them, the other is inaccessible. Nothing meaningful can be said about it. The fact that a religious language is unavoidable means the contamination of pure religion. According to Boeve, this concept results in a committed agnosticism.[20] It favours, indeed, behaving *etsi Deus daretur*, however, without knowing whether the addressee is present. In the end, we fall prey to a kind of negative theology without exit again. Moreover, it all seems to be another

---

[16] Jean-Luc Marion, *God without Being: Hors-texte* (Chicago, Il: The University of Chicago Press, 1995).

[17] Richard Kearney, *The God Who May Be: The Hermeneutics of Religion* (Bloomington, IN: Indiana University Press, 2002), p. 31.

[18] Lieven Boeve, "Theological Truth, Particularity and Incarnation: Engaging Religious Plurality and Radical Hermeneutics," in *Orthodoxy, Process and Product*, ed. Mathijs Lamberigts, Lieven Boeve and Terrence Merrigan, Bibliotheca Ephemeridum theologicarum Lovaniensium 227 (Leuven: Peeters, 2009), p. 337.

[19] John D. Caputo, *On Religion* (London, New York: Routledge, 2001), pp. 109–141.

[20] Cf. Lieven Boeve, "Theological Truth in the Context of Contemporary Continental Thought: The Turn to Religion and the Contamination of Language," in *The Question of Theological Truth: Philosophical and Interreligious Perspectives*, ed. Frederiek Depoortere and Magdalen Lambkin, (Amsterdam, New York: Rodopi, 2012), pp. 77–100.

philosophical variation on the paradigm of religious pluralism.[21] Particular religious traditions represent the contamination of the original religion which is to be found beyond all of them. Theologically speaking, we leave seekers twisting in the wind.

Richard Kearney criticizes such inevitably negative theologies. In his book *Strangers, Gods and Monsters*,[22] he argues that such a wholly inaccessible otherness might create, as the title indicates, terrible counterfeits of God. Kearney's attempt to make Christianity understandable in postmodern conditions is dependent upon his reinterpretation of Ex 3:14. Usual English translations read this phrase: "I am who I am."[23] Instead of the onto-theological reading insisting on the verb *esse* in the present tense, Kearney proposes an alternative interpretation focusing on the future: "I will be who I will be." Kearney's God, *who may be*, is a God engaged in history.[24] How to speak about this strange God? Kearney suggests the way of *anatheism* – "a third way between the extremes of dogmatic theism and militant atheism."[25] Anatheism is a wager on faith which is open to dark nights, doubt and uncertainty. Thus, for Kearny, it seems to be more important to *have* faith instead of *naming* faith. This risk may result in a more mature and committed faith, but also it may end up in a hopeless agnosticism or even atheism. The darkness might evoke deep mystical experiences, or anxiety and despair. In short, we are balancing on the edges between faith and non-faith. Perhaps this is the right point where the Church needs to dwell for a while in order to appeal to seekers.

But there is still the question whether Kearney, like other postmodern thinkers, does not dismiss religious language too quickly. Aren't we still locked in negations? It makes sense that after modern attempts to apply *clear and distinct* ideas in the speech of God, postmodern authors recuperate negative theology in their respective thinking of God. They want to emphasize genuine otherness and its inexpressibility. For postmodernists, God is hidden, incomprehensible,

---

[21] Cf. Gavin D'Costa, *Christianity and World Religions: Disputed Questions in the Theology of Religions* (Malden, MA: Wiley-Blackwell, 2009), pp. 9–12. Although D'Costa does not refer to the aforementioned postmodern authors, his description of pluralism resembles to the main arguments of philosophy of deconstruction with regard to religion.

[22] Richard Kearney, *Strangers, Gods, and Monsters: Ideas of Otherness* (London, New York: Routledge, 2003).

[23] This way reads NRSV and NAS. KJV reads similar: "I am that I am."

[24] Kearney, *The God Who May Be*, pp. 1–8.

[25] Richard Kearney, *Anatheism: Returning to God after God* (New York: Columbia University Press, 2010), p. 3.

absent.[26] This sense of otherness is in some way very correct and reveals something true. It cannot, however, be applied in theological-philosophical discourse one-sidedly. What if all the attempts to avoid the naming of faith are wrong and, at the end, misleading? What if we can neither purify religious language, nor perfect it? What if the only acceptable way, at least the only way for Christian theology, is to enjoy the crisis of language?

THE CRISIS OF RELIGIOUS LANGUAGE

Rowan Williams suggests that authentic religious language is always under pressure.[27] According to this significant Welch theologian, there are three basic modes of what might be called the habit of speaking about God: (1) The mode of superficial invoking of God in non-religious situations such as "where is the God bloody hammer; God knows; oh my God," etc. (2) A classical religious speech which can be found in catechisms, sermons, among disputing believers, the speech grounded in prescriptions, sanctions, "yes-no" answers. In short, a descriptive mode of language removes all the mystery of God's being for the sake of our understanding. Nevertheless, there is still one more possibility: (3) the language of God as a creative uncertainty and inescapability. In other words, the language is put under pressure; the language has reached its limits. Williams argues that it is only in the third case where we engage with genuine religious language. Or we can put it conversely: language becomes religious only under pressure.

Williams reminds us that language is not just a system of stimulus and response. We cannot really control or predict the reply in language. We can agree with Jean-François Lyotard that the phrase *a* always provokes a responding phrase.[28] However, whether it will be the phrase *b, c, d,* or *x* or perhaps even the phrase of silence, nobody can control. In religious language, there is no last word. Arguably, this is an eternal temptation of human beings, the temptation to have the last word, to

---

[26] Cf. Lieven Boeve, "The Rediscovery of Negative Theology Today: The Narrow Gulf between Theology and Philosophy," in *Théologie négative*, ed. Marco M. Olivetti, Biblioteca dell'Archivio di filosofia (Padova: CEDAM, 2002), pp. 446–447.

[27] Cf. Rowan Williams, "Making Representations: Religious Faith and the Habits of Language" (The University of Edinburgh, November 04, 2013), https://www.youtube.com/playlist?list=PLEA9467E8E8D991AE, accessed November 24, 2013.

[28] Cf. Jean-François Lyotard, *The Different: Phrases in Dispute* (Manchester: Manchester University Press, 1988), pp. xi-xvi and 135-145.

possess an exhaustive answer and reach the point when nothing more can be said. Interestingly, religious people suffer from this ambition more than any other people. Fortunately, it is not possible to remove language from its crisis. There is always something more to be said.

One possible way of how to put language under pressure is to question. Tomáš Halík, a Czech theologian and philosopher, elaborates on this topic in relation to Kearney's ideas. Besides the metaphor of a God who may be, Halík identifies perhaps a more appealing one for how to address the question of God in the current context. He proposes to reconsider the notion of *an unknown God* (Acts 17:23).[29] The current state of affairs resembles the situation of those who were listening to Paul on Areopagus. Many seekers ask what the Christian teaching is about. "Who is your God?" Instead of the catechism definitions, Halík suggests to direct our eyes at the altar of an unknown God.

However, with regard to the position of seekers, we must ask the following questions: (i) Is it possible to communicate Christian faith to someone who is not familiar with the symbolic language of Christianity? (ii) May we consider the experience with *an unknown God* as an authentic experience with God without anchoring it in some narrative about God?

The methodological distinction between the strategies *ad intra* as well as *ad extra*, proposed in section 1, does not help here. Seekers are neither fully inside the Church, nor outside of it. Seekers stand in the middle, in between the Church and the others. They are both the others as well as those among us. They are in the between (*in medio*). What is most needed might be therefore called a strategy of the middle–*in medio*. Seekers are culturally familiar with the Christian narrative because Christianity is still present in the European culture (e.g. architecture, literature, art).[30] Seekers are explicitly sympathetic towards the Christian

---

[29] This concept is unpacked in chapter VI of this volume (Martin Kočí and Pavel Roubík, "An Unknown God of Paradox: Tomáš Halík on Faith in a Secular Age") which is dedicated solely to Halík's theological contribution to the current theological-philosophical debate in a secular age.

[30] I think of my home town of Prague. Although Prague is the capital of one of the most secular countries in Europe, Christianity is present at every corner. The citizens might not be conscious about it, but they live in the midst of Christian symbols and signs of many kinds. This, of course, forms their world-views. Thus, this cultural presence of Christianity might be one of the causes why we meet so many seekers in a postmodern age. Halík expresses something similar: "We cannot fail to notice the presence of faith in all places where the biblical message shape culture and the relationship of human beings to the world. In the Euro-Atlantic spiritual space, we find the Christian faith at every corner and even beyond the borders of 'religion'." Tomáš Halík, *Žít s*

interpretation of the world. The question is how to communicate faith to them. Halík says that "God reveals himself in questions."[31] The questions asked by seekers, the questions directed at an unknown God, might be a new way of the presenting God – the way *in medio*.

The fact that God becomes something of a stranger is not necessarily an impasse. Moreover, this does not apply only for seekers but also for dwellers. The current crisis is not a threat, as Halík often reminds us. Rather it is a chance to open new ways of understanding God and interpreting the role of Christianity in the world. The paradox of seekers, who are simultaneously inside and outside, exposes the fragility of religious language. It shows that our God-talk cannot be final and comprehensive. It is always provisional. Furthermore, to approach seekers does not imply to turn them to dwellers. According to Halík, the question is stated in a different way. Does the Church offer some space for seekers, while simultaneously allowing them to remain seekers?

In my opinion, the aforementioned Williams suggests a reasonable way in a contemporary context. He insists that we put language under pressure in order to discover more.[32] Think of science, literature, philosophy, and poetry. In all these realms we deliberately make things more difficult in order to go deeper. Why should theology be withdrawn from this perplexing marvel of language? In fact, the traditional theology has ever been witnessing the beauty of crisis in naming God. For example, the creed, dogmas, and of course, Scripture itself is language under pressure. Seekers questioning God must know that what the Church believes is a true language but also inadequate. The words of naming God used by the traditional confessions of the Church are the best words one can probably find, but it must be clear that these words, at the same time, fall short. To put it differently, the task of the Church, while communicating with seekers, is not only to put religious language under pressure but also to show the pressure *within* language itself. "If I am showing that it is difficult to talk about God, I am showing the truth about God."[33]

The words we use for telling the story of God are never enough. There is always something missing. The task of theology is not to cover the gap. On the contrary, theology must unveil this gap; i.e. the difficulty

---

tajemstvím: Podněty k promýšlení víry (Praha: Nakladatelství Lidové noviny: 2013), p. 18.

[31] Tomáš Halík, *Chci, abys byl: Křesťanství po náboženství* (Praha: Nakladatelství Lidové noviny, 2012), p. 15.

[32] Rowan Williams, "Religious Language under Pressure" (Radboud University Nijmegen, December 13, 2013).

[33] Ibid.

of language about God in order to be truthful about God. It is a hard task to speak about God. It is a hard task to communicate faith. The Church must not be embarrassed to confess that to speak of God is both a matter of excitement and trauma.

What about to move on even a step further. It seems reasonable to suggest a new strategy – an inverse strategy complementary to the preceding theological outline. A first question, for the Church's part, should not be what dwellers can say to seekers about God, but what seekers may say about God to dwellers. The issue at stake is not to teach seekers how to dwell in the Church. On the contrary, dwellers must join seekers, dwell among them for a while, and thus learn how to seek God. Halík curiously reverses a liturgical dialogue between the priest and catechumen which takes place right before the act of baptism. A traditional order reads as follows. Priest: "What do you ask from the Church?" Catechumen replies: "Knowing Christ." Priest continues: "Why do you want to know Christ?" Catechumen: "To become his disciple." Halík's proposes a different ordering. It is seekers beyond the borders of the Church who pose the question: "What do you want from us?" Christians should listen to them carefully and then respond: "Knowing Christ." Seekers, however, might continue: "Why do you want to know Christ?" The answer is: "To become his disciples."[34] Indeed, it is seekers who show that "each Christian is a *homo viator* and the Church is the *communio viatorum*."[35]

CONCLUSION

What is the lesson from a postmodern quest? When we wrestle with the ambiguity of religious language, we should avoid the temptation of explanation. Rather, our struggle must evoke a perplexing, yet marvellous experience of standing in front of mystery; both *tremendum et fascinans*, as Rudolf Otto aptly puts it. Religious language is not meant to clear things but to evoke the event of the living God. This is what the Christian tradition is about: "as a whole... is this continuing process of the conversion of human language to God."[36]

What is then our problem? Is it only a matter of language? I dare to say, the problem is the loss of wisdom. Postmodern thinkers criticise modern rationalism and they are right in many respects. They

---

[34] Tomáš Halík, *Divadlo pro anděly: Život jako náboženský experiment* (Praha: Nakladatelství Lidové noviny, 2010), pp. 146-147.

[35] Tomáš Halík, *Stromu zbývá naděje: Krize jako šance* (Praha: Nakladatelství Lidové noviny, 2009), p. 200.

[36] Myers, *Christ the Stranger*, p. 35.

deconstruct a monstrous creature of modern rationality. They might, however, forget a constructive path of wisdom. It does not mean to go back before modernity. We have to find a new unity in our – postmodern – way. Perhaps those who are *in the middle* are tired of deconstruction and afraid of the way back the Church seems to promote. They are hungry for a new unity, for wisdom in a postmodern way.

> Wisdom, the Greeks said, is the love of the highest things, all of them, the true, the good and the beautiful. It includes reason without stopping at reason; it includes truth but it does not reduce truth to that which is established by reason, and it does not exclude the good and the beautiful from the true. The true, the good and the beautiful hang together.
>
> Wisdom included insight and intuition as well as definitions and arguments (the true); it included action, living well, ethical and political wisdom (the good), not just professional knowledge; and it included Plato's idea that a life surrounded by beautiful things promotes the beauty of the soul (the beautiful).[37]

Perhaps Halík points out a possible solution. It is neither a change of external structures, nor an accommodation to a current culture. We have to move into the depth. It is about our ability to be authentically particular (not exclusive). In this context, Halík's proposal that the Church should recontextualize itself into a shape of the medieval university makes sense. On the ground of the university, every question is permitted. Such an ecclesiological model would allow space for those *in medio* and preserve the Church to be a place where the Christian particularity is confirmed, yet not absolute. It would be a porous particularity but still a particularity without embarrassment. In practice, the Church must go out of the temple and enter into the courtyard of nations (seekers). The Church must seek God with seekers.

BIBLIOGRAPHY

Boeve, Lieven. 2002. "The Rediscovery of Negative Theology Today: The Narrow Gulf between Theology and Philosophy." In *Théologie négative*. Edited by Marco M. Olivetti, 443-59. Biblioteca dell'Archivio di filosofia. Padova: CEDAM.

---

[37] John D. Caputo, *Truth* (London: Penguin Books), pp. 23-24.

———. 2007. *God Interrupts History: Theology in a Time of Upheaval*. New York: Continuum.

———. 2009. "Theological Truth, Particularity and Incarnation: Engaging Religious Plurality and Radical Hermeneutics." In *Orthodoxy, Process and Product*. Edited by Mathijs Lamberigts, Lieven Boeve and Terrence Merrigan, 323-48. Bibliotheca Ephemeridum theologicarum Lovaniensium 227. Leuven: Peeters.

———. 2011. "Communicating Faith in Contemporary Europe: Dealing with Language Problems in and outside the Church." In *Communicating Faith*. Edited by John Sullivan, 293-308. Washington, D.C: Catholic University of America Press.

———. 2012. "Theological Truth in the Context of Contemporary Continental Thought: The Turn to Religion and the Contamination of Language." In *The Question of Theological Truth: Philosophical and Interreligious Perspectives*. Edited by Frederiek Depoortere and Magdalen Lambkin, 77–100. Currents of encounter 46. Amsterdam, New York: Rodopi.

Caputo, John D. 2001. *On Religion*. Thinking in action. London, New York: Routledge.

———. 2013. *Truth*. Philosophy in transit. London: Penguin Books.

D'Costa, Gavin. 2009. *Christianity and World Religions: Disputed Questions in the Theology of Religions*. Chichester, U.K, Malden, Mass: Wiley-Blackwell.

Depoortere, Frederiek and Magdalen Lambkin. (eds.), 2012. *The Question of Theological Truth: Philosophical and Interreligious Perspectives*. Currents of encounter 46. Amsterdam, New York: Rodopi.

Halík, Tomáš. 2009. *Patience with God: The Story of Zacchaeus Continuing in Us*. New York: Doubleday.

Kearney, Richard. 2002. *The God Who May Be: The Hermeneutics of Religion*. Bloomington, IN: Indiana University Press.

———. 2003. *Strangers, Gods, and Monsters: Ideas of Otherness*. London, New York: Routledge.

———. 2010. *Anatheism: Returning to God after God*. Insurrections. New York: Columbia University Press.

Lamberigts, Mathijs, Lieven Boeve, and Terrence Merrigan. (eds.), 2009. *Orthodoxy, Process and Product*. Bibliotheca Ephemeridum theologicarum Lovaniensium 227. Leuven: Peeters.

Lash, Nicholas. 2004. *Holiness, Speech and Silence: Reflections on the Question of God*. Aldershot, Burlington, VT: Ashgate Pub.

Lyotard, Jean-François. 1984. *The Postmodern Condition: A Report on Knowledge*. Minneapolis: University of Minnesota Press.

———. 1988. *The Differend: Phrases in Dispute*. Manchester: Manchester University Press.

Marion, Jean-Luc. 1995. *God without Being: Hors-texte.* Religion and postmodernism. Chicago, Il: The University of Chicago Press.

Myers, Benjamin. 2012. *Christ the Stranger: The Theology of Rowan Williams.* London, New York: T & T Clark.

Olivetti, Marco M. (ed.), 2002. *Théologie négative.* Biblioteca dell'Archivio di filosofia. Padova: CEDAM.

Sullivan, John. (ed.), 2011. *Communicating Faith.* Washington, D.C: Catholic University of America Press.

Taylor, Charles. 2012. "The Church Speak – To Whom?" In *Church and People: Disjunctions in a Secular Age.* Edited by Charles Taylor, José Casanova and George F. McLean, 17–24. Cultural heritage and contemporary change. Series 8. Christian philosophical studies 1. Washington, D.C.: Council for Research in Values and Philosophy.

Taylor, Charles, José Casanova, and George F. McLean. (eds.), 2012. *Church and People: Disjunctions in a Secular Age.* Cultural heritage and contemporary change. Series 8. Christian philosophical studies 1. Washington, D.C.: Council for Research in Values and Philosophy.

Williams, Rowan. 2013. "Making Representations: Religious Faith and the Habits of Language." The University of Edinburgh, November 04, 2013. Accessed online November 24, 2013. https://www.youtube.com/playlist?list=PLEA9467E8E8D991AE.

———, 2013 "Religious Language under Pressure." Radboud University Nijmegen, December 13.

CHAPTER VI

SEARCHING THE ALTAR OF AN UNKNOWN GOD: TOMÁŠ HALÍK ON FAITH IN A SECULAR AGE

MARTIN KOČÍ AND *PAVEL ROUBÍK*

INTRODUCTION

Religion has always been a dynamic phenomenon. From a contextual theological perspective, the last century was full of turbulent changes on the European continent. What was a hundred years ago a highly religious culture, is today rather an indifferent and even religiously ignorant society. Nobody can doubt that the meaning of religion and religious identity has changed significantly. We got accustomed to call this process of changes *secularization*. Yet there are various different interpretations of this phenomenon. Some thinkers, for example, welcome secularization as a liberation of human beings from the bonds of religion.[1] Other authors approach secularization with sympathy because they believe it helps to purify institutional religions. Finally, there are those who oppose secularization and look for ways in which to stop this process or to reverse it. Many important studies on the topic of secularization and, consequently, on the changed conditions of faith have been published in recent years. One of the shining examples of such works is Charles Taylor's ground-breaking voluminous study *A Secular Age*.[2] One of the numerous merits of Taylor's work is that he points out clearly how and in what sense the theme of secularization is both a trauma and challenge for theologians, philosophers of religion and sociologists.

We dare to dedicate this chapter to an author who openly confesses that he feels to be "crucified between the paradoxes" of the

---

[1] Social anthropologist Anthony F. C. Wallace expresses such a conviction quite bluntly: "[T]he evolutionary future of religion is extinction. Belief in supernatural forces that affect nature without obeying nature's laws will erode and become only an interesting historical memory." Anthony F. C. Wallace, *Religion: An Anthropological View* (New York: Random House, 1966), pp. 264-265.

[2] Charles Taylor, *A Secular Age* (Cambridge, MT: Harvard University Press, 2007).

secular world and the world of religion. We will present an author who struggles with both faith and doubts. Furthermore, this author lives in one of the most secularized countries in Europe. His experience of being on the edges of belief and unbelief, the Church and the world leads him to an original (re)interpretation of secularization in particular and the current state of religion in general. The main subject of this study is to introduce this remarkable person, the Czech theologian, sociologist and philosopher Tomáš Halík.

We will divide this chapter into three parts. Firstly, we will outline Halík's description of the contemporary religious situation in Europe with special attention paid to the issue of secularization and its development in recent decades. We will work solely with Halík's ideas which at first sight seem to be rather eclectic, however, a closer engagement with them reveals numerous original insights formulated on the background of both contemporary theological-philosophical-sociological thought and a specific experience with a highly secular context, which is at the same time quite open to religious questions.[3] This interesting interaction between secular and at the same time implicitly religious cultural strata will be pointed out in the second part of this chapter. To better illustrate Halík's position, we will highlight some specific characteristics of the Czech cultural context. Thirdly, we will test our hypothesis that Halík's thought leads to an original theological contribution which may help the Church to renew itself in contemporary postmodern context.

VOCATUS ET NONVOCATUS: **EUROPE IN A SECULAR AGE**

The post-Enlightenment development changed the religious map of Europe. Analogously to the situation after the destruction of the Temple in Jerusalem, resulting in the rise of the two branches of an older religion in the Holy Land, modernity gave birth to the two competing cultures from the rubble of medieval *Christianitas*: the culture of the modern ecclesial Christianity and *Laïcité* – the modern lay secular culture. The former shaped quasi-ideological structures not dissimilar to the political and social movements of modernity. Next to Liberalism, Capitalism, and Socialism Catholicism and Protestantism appeared as other *–isms*. This internal development of Christianity has caused a paradigm change in the Christian tradition. *Laïcité* on the other hand developed its own specific form of religiosity implicitly present in

---

[3] When we refer to other authorities, the purpose is to enlighten or to elaborate on Halík's arguments.

general culture as an "alternative" to the feuding camps of Catholics and Protestants.[4] In many respects, secular culture under the flag of *laïcité* represents "a heterodox form of Christianity" but "it stays not outside but inside the broad historical stream of Christianity."[5] Arguably, there are two versions of Christianity which, in the words of Chesterton, tend to go crazy: *popular* (religion as *pietas*) and *intellectual* (religion as a spiritual-humanistic philosophy). Intellectual religion leads most often to agnosticism and subsequently to atheism, whereas "*pietas* religion" tends to take the form of new religious movements.[6]

The consequence of this complicated development has been gradual mutual alienation of the Christian and the lay culture. Moreover, a secular culture began to be superior in numbers and, after all, the non-Churched laity has won Europe culturally and politically. The winning side was strongly linked to the modern natural science that – having replaced theology – has become "the language of the modern elite and the arbiter of truth."[7] Halík aptly summarizes the situation as the defeat of traditional Christianity which was replaced by a modern religion.

The ecclesial Christianity responded in two unfortunate ways: liberalism and traditionalism/fundamentalism. Liberalism proclaims that the relationship between Christianity and the prevailing culture must be considered in terms of continuity. In contrast, fundamentalism postulates an unbridgeable gap between *societas terrena* (secular world) and *societas perfecta* (the ecclesial type of Christianity). Although the so-called correlation theology, an heir of the former, makes a lot of effort to translate Christian language into secular terms and survives till these days, the latter have proved to be stronger. From the turn of the 19th and 20th century when the anti-modernist fight flared up, through the opposition to any sort of openness to contemporary culture about the time of Vatican II, to the late pontificate of Benedict XVI, the spectre of traditionalism haunts the Christian Church.

Halík harshly criticizes this tendency, evident especially in the first half of the 20th century and its respective outcomes nowadays: "Anxiety caused by the loss of political and cultural positions and the status of the intellectual elite did not lead the Church nobility to a self-critical search for real causes of this state of affairs but to a paranoic 'witch-hunt' in which the Church forfeited many of its best minds through intimidation, persecution and psychological pressure. Thus the

---

[4] Cf. Tomáš Halík, "Křesťanství a laicita," *Universum* 1 (2013), pp. 17-19; here p. 18.
[5] Tomáš Halík, *Vzýván i nevzýván* (Praha: Lidové noviny, 2004), p. 61.
[6] Halík, *Vzýván i nevzýván*, p. 55.
[7] Halík, "Křesťanství a laicita," p. 18.

Church intellectually castrated itself to a large extent. This self-undoing tendency would gradually bring the Church into the position of a marginal obscure sect at the edge of society"[8] Vatican II, in Halík's opinion, fortunately interrupted this defensive mentality resulting in hostility towards the secular world. Since the modern paradigm shift, for the Catholic Church, Vatican II represents the first serious attempt to step out of *Catholicism* to *Catholicity* and thus an attempt to recontextualize the notion of *Christianitas* by leaving the notion of *societas perfecta* behind.

For Halík, Vatican II is a step towards a renewed relationship between the Church and secular culture. This is, however, possible only under the condition that the Church moves beyond the modern kind of oppositional thinking. Thus Halík offers a sort of postmodern critique of the phenomenon of Catholicism as a product of modernity and the modern mentality. According to Halík, the term '*Catholic-ism*' refers to a particular historical form of the Catholic tradition. The Church developed into a closed ghetto and counter-cultural system against the modern world. Metaphorically expressed, the Church in the period of modernity is more like a fortress with high walls than a mother with open embracing arms.[9] '*Catholic-ism*' built up a 'parallel world' which caused the Catholic Church to move to the margins of society. "Instead of offering spirituality and mysticism, Christianity offered moral commands and interdicts. Instead of initiation to the mysteries of faith, memorizing the catechism was imposed. Instead of spiritual leadership, submissiveness to the Church authority was requested."[10] Thus Catholicism developed a coherent Catholic system in order to build up a secure place in a Godless world. A defensive mentality created an ideological system not dissimilar to other modern ideologies. Paradoxically, the aggressive orientation of the Church resulted in the acceptance of certain aspects of modern logic. Halík mentions the example of a disproportionate emphasis on the papacy and papal authority (*ultramontanism*) strikingly reminiscent of the political power of the modern national state. In theology, the shift from Thomism to Neo-Thomism ended up in accepting the logic of modern rationalism

---

[8] Halík, "Křesťanství a laicita," p. 18.

[9] "Horrifying evidence of the mentality of the late modern era is the 'Syllabus Errorum' published by Pius IX; likewise the combat against modernism which degenerated into the paranoid spying and bureaucratic bullying of many honest theologians." Tomáš Halík, *Co je bez chvění, není pevné* (Praha: Lidové noviny, 2002), p. 153.

[10] Tomáš Halík, *Stromu zbývá naděje: Krize jako šance* (Praha: Lidové noviny, 2009), p. 48.

(*clare et distincte*). In order to illustrate what the logic of '*Catholic-ism*' is, Halík highlights the famous statement of Pius XI: 'against any political party we will establish a Catholic party, against any association we will establish a Catholic association, and against any publisher we will establish a Catholic publisher.'[11] The ideological system of Catholicism entered the war against the ideological system of humanism, atheism, socialism, liberalism, scientific positivism, and even Protestantism etc. Without irony, Halík praises secularization (which in an important sense has been acknowledged by Vatican II), as a deliverance from the aforementioned mentality of Catholicism and as a factor that helped to pave the way for *Catholicity* as an authentic form of the Church in the contemporary context. This authentic form is not based on restoration of any previous form of the Church, neither is it based on any cheap adaptation to current culture. Catholicity rather includes a universal openness in line with the Biblical notion of openness and the Patristic theological principle *ecclesia semper reformanda*.[12] In this respect, Halík believes that the Pauline heritage is of crucial importance. The theology of the apostle Paul opens Christianity to other contexts outside of the Jewish world. Paul shows that Christianity is not a religion analogous to Judaism or Roman cults. The Christian Church must be a permanently open community. Christianity must develop a community entering into new contexts and accepting new possibilities of theological reflection.[13] "Catholicity (universality, completeness) means 'openness'. The Church living out its Catholicity is the Church striving for openness to all. Catholicity is related to the miracle of Pentecost, speaking in all languages."[14]

It is worth mentioning that for Halík the term *Catholicity* is is not a confessional designation.[15] Catholic identity should imply a different meaning than for example, a Marxist identity. The adjective 'Catholic' is not an ideological brand of some kind of closed narrative. Catholic tradition is continually undergoing interruptions of permanent crisis.

---

[11] An inquiry into historical documents does not confirm Halík's ascription of this quote to Pius XI. As a matter of fact we have found this quote in the text of the Czech bishop Brynych (1846-1902). Cf. M. Kovář, "Biskup Edna a Jan Nep. Brynych," *Sborník historického kroužku* 1 (1903), pp. 1-3; here p. 1.

[12] Cf. Halík, *Vzýván i nevzýván*, pp. 223-224.

[13] Cf. Halík, *Stromu zbývá naděje*, p. 84-85.

[14] Halík, *Vzýván i nevzýván*, p. 234.

[15] "To be a Catholic does not mean a strict affiliation with one of many Christian denominations. Rather, it is the commitment to work for the universal openness of the Church." Halík, *Vzýván i nevzýván*, p. 251.

Catholic identity should always be initiating, creative, responsible, and open until the coming of the eschaton. In other words, Catholicity must be universally open to questions from academia and society in order to permanently recontextualize itself.[16]

Analogously to the previous distinction between *Catholicity* and *Catholicism*, Halík distinguishes between *secularization* and *secularism*.[17] The former is the outcome of Christianity. It functions as a purification of faith and thus demands a responsible Christian identity within a changing world. The latter, on the contrary, designates the ideology of "neutral objectivity" deduced from the modern positivist logic. Consequently, secularism leads to individualism with the crypto-metaphysical doctrine of materialism.[18] The emphasis on secularization in contrast to secularism, analogously to the counter-poles of Catholicity and Catholicism, demonstrates Halík's quest for the theological thinking paradigm between the Scylla of ideological religious triumphalism and the Charybdis of ideological secularism. In this sense we can say that Halík belongs to the diverse group of postmodern authors who strive to recover whatever is holy and noble in both religion and culture.

Halík, for example, sympathizes with the postmodern philosopher Gianni Vattimo who claims that secularization is a specific form of Christianity.[19] Halík formulates an interesting question about whether secularization could be interpreted as a realization of Christ's *kenosis* (i.e. self-emptying). Furthermore, Halík asks whether the process of secularization could be understood as a step forward in the development of Christian tradition in the postmodern context.[20] Halík suggests that the essential element of secularization is the fight against corrupt forms of religion in the public square. This endeavour is based on internal elements of the Christian tradition: i) the biblical ethos of the

---

[16] For Halík, a (Catholic) university is an optimum place for the realization of such identity. Consequently, the mission of (Catholic) universities includes promoting a genuine universality and a genuine openness. Cf. *Vzýván i nevzýván*, p. 238.

[17] He accepts the distinction made by the German theologian F. Gogarten, the founder of the so-called 'theology of secularization'. Friedrich Gogarten, *Verhängnis und Hoffnung der Neuzeit. Die Säkularisierung als theologisches Problem* (Stuttgart: Friedrich Vorwerk, 1953).

[18] Cf. Halík, *Vzýván i nevzýván*, pp. 118-119.

[19] Cf. Gianni Vattimo, *Belief* (Cambridge: Polity Press, 1999), pp. 46-48.

[20] Cf. Tomáš Halík, *Patience with God: The Story of Zaccheus Continuing in Us* (New York: Doubleday, 2009), pp. 39-43; Halík, *Vzýván i nevzýván*, 9. In fact, Halík claims to be the first one to raise such a question of secularization as the next stage in the development of the Latin Christian tradition. Cf. *ibid.*, p. 347.

desacralisation of nature and politics clearly expressed in the Hebrew Bible and in the New Testament; (ii) the division of the secular and ecclesial spheres as a consequence of the Investiture Controversy in the Middle-Ages; (iii) Christian humanist attempts to establish a non-confessional alternative to the warring camps of Protestants and Catholics in the early modern era. The modern era has arisen on the Christian foundations somewhat "naturally". The disappearance of Christianity from European culture does not turn Europe into atheistic or non-religious entity. Rather, Europe has become "religious" in a different way when compared with the classical understanding.

What is the role of the Church in this new European cultural setting? According to Halík, the Church faces an important but difficult task to be just the Church. It is quite obvious that various world-views show a permanent tendency to deteriorate into ideologies. This happens to be the case with some religious and some secular narratives as well.[21] The Church ought to consciously fight against this omnipresent and eternal temptation. The Church has an uneasy task to "*prevent the secular culture from becoming a para-religion.* The secular culture of the West is really secular and nonreligious to the extent to which it is Christian."[22] Europe has two faces: the Christian and the secular. How should we arrange the coexistence of both, similar yet different faces, in the same area? A polite tolerance is certainly not enough. An unmediated opposition is counter-productive. The Church, for its part, must go further. Halík puts it boldly: "The future of Europe lies in finding a dynamic compatibility between two European traditions: the Christian one and the secular-humanistic one."[23]

The Parable of the Prodigal Son might be interpreted in a new way in light of what has been said above. Christianity and secular humanist culture are "brothers" since they have the same mother, Europe, and the same grandparents, the Jewish faith and ancient wisdom. However, thinking of contemporary Christianity in relation to the secular culture we tend to forget that there is also the same father, the

---

[21] Using the term 'Western civilization' or simply the 'West', Halík means Euro-Atlantic civilization which grew up from Christian tradition which is itself based on the encounter of Jewish faith and ancient Greek philosophy and Roman law, however, interrupted by the Reformation and Enlightenment. Cf. Halík, *Co je bez chvění*, p. 173.

[22] Tomáš Halík, *Divadlo pro anděly: Život jako náboženský experiment* (Praha: Lidové noviny 2010), p. 131.

[23] Tomáš Halík, *Chci, abys byl. Křesťanství po náboženství* (Praha: Lidové noviny, 2012), p. 26.

Enlightenment.[24] However much Christians refer to ancient authorities such as St. Augustine, or St. Thomas Aquinas, their reading of them cannot but be through post-Enlightenment lens and we dare to add through postmodern lens as well.[25] Halík is strongly convinced of his postmodern enlightened belief: "When Christianity takes secular humanism seriously and embrace it as its brother, contemporary secular culture will be able to take Christianity seriously."[26]

The meeting between Christianity and secularization has caused two things. Firstly, Christianity no longer functions as the integrative element of Western society. Secondly, secularization functions as an "interruption" of ecclesial and institutional Christianity. The process of secularization reveals a crisis of both pre-modern religion mirroring the form of ancient *religio*, and modern religion emphasising the confessional-institutional nature of religious identity. Thus, according to Halík, the process of secularization results in the definitive divorce between Christian faith, the ancient concept of *religio* as an integrative force in society and the modern concept of a closed religious narrative.[27] Secularization, therefore, is not the process of de-Christianization of society. It just forces Christianity to recontextualize itself into a new shape. In other words, Halík emphasizes the same thing as Charles Taylor does in his recent *opus magnum*; i.e. secularization is, above all, about the changed conditions of faith.[28] In other words, what we face in

---

[24] Cf. Halík, *Patience with God*, pp. 83-84.

[25] For example the Radical Orthodoxy movement claims to go back to the pre-modern form of Christianity. This strategy is, however, based on certain (postmodern) presuppositions which would have been impossible without Kant, so to say.

[26] Halík, *Chci, abys byl*, p. 229.

[27] Cf. Halík, *Co je bez chvění*, pp. 160-161.

[28] In addition to that, Halík develops also the ideas of T. Luckmann, particularly his theory of secularization as a process of individualization and privatization of religion which becomes "invisible" (cf. Thomas Luckmann, *The invisible Religion: The Problem of Religion in Modern Society* [New York: Maxmillan 1967]) and P. L. Berger's identification of the roots of secularization as genuinely Western and secularization as "pluralisation" (cf. Peter L. Berger and Thomas Luckmann, *The Social Construction of Reality: A Treatise in the Sociology of Knowledge* [Harmondsworth: Penguin Books, 1971]; Peter L. Berger, *A Far Glory: The Quest for Faith in an Age of Credulity* [New York: Free Press, 1992]). Similarly to the aforementioned thinkers, Halík is convinced that man is *homo religiosus*. Friedrich D. E. Schleiermacher, the "Church father of the 19th century" (so first Hermann Weiß), postulates besides the metaphysical and moral realms also the *religious area* in human mind. Cf. Friedrich D. E. Schleiermacher, *Über die Religion: Reden an die Gebildeten*

the current era is the change of religious *forms*, but *not its contents*.[29] Nonetheless, the alienation from a certain type of Christian culture opens space for a new contextual form of Christianity. The crisis does not affect religion as such but certain religious language strategies which are not contextually plausible and theological valid anymore.[30] To put it differently, the process of secularization is one particular form of Christian heritage in Europe and at the same time a sort of recontextualisation of Christian tradition.

"A spectre is haunting Europe, the spectre of religion," says Halík in paraphrasing Marx's famous quote.[31] Despite all possible assumptions, the process of secularization does not result in a non-religious society. Only certain forms of religion are weakened. But faith remains and looks for new ways of expression.[32] This is almost a common sense fact among contemporary theologians and sociologists of religion. However, the situation of postmodernity is ambiguous. Many are obsessed with discussing God, religion, and moral values. Some people want to expel religion from the public square into a private sphere and still tell the story of modernity as an emancipation from religion.[33] Others call for preservation of the closed confessional character of Christian tradition in accordance with the modern story.

---

unter ihren Verächtern (1799), G. Meckenstock (ed.) (Berlin/New York: de Gruyter, 1999), § 37 (according to the first edition), p. 72. Halík finds religion to be a *conditio humana*. "I try to explain to people that religion does not solely concern those people who think God exist.... The sphere of religion, in the broad and basic meaning of the expression, is as fundamental and natural a part of human life as the ethical, the aesthetic, or the erotic, and just as in the case of those areas of life, it can have a different connotation and orientation for specific individuals, and there are different degrees to which it can be cultivated or, alternatively, neglected and undeveloped." Tomáš Halík, *Night of the Confessor: Christian Faith in an Age of Uncertainty* (New York: Image Books/Doubleday, 2012), p. 118.

[29] Cf. Tomáš Halík, "Katolická církev v České republice po roce 1989," in *Společnost v přerodu* (Praha: Masarykův ústav AV ČR, 2000), p. 146.

[30] Halík, "Katolická církev v České republice po roce 1989," 153. For example, a banal image of God is no more credible. Cf. Halík, *Chci, abys byl*, 84.

[31] Halík, *Vzýván i nevzýván*, 321.

[32] Cf. Tomáš Halík, "Globalizace a náboženství," in *Globalizace*, Václav Mezřický (ed.) (Praha: Portál, 2003), pp. 133-147.

[33] For example, the proponents of the so-called "New Atheism" such as Richard Dawkins, Daniel Dennett, and Christopher Hitchens, a. o.

Others even try to persuade contemporary society that pre-modern *Christianitas* was the ideal form of European civilization.[34]

Halík's analysis, however, shows that contemporary Christianity is neither *religio* with its integrative power,[35] nor a cultural phenomenon in the modern sense. In Halík's opinion, Christian identity primarily means having an individual and particular identity in a pluralistic society.[36] Belonging or not belonging to a particular tradition is not easily transmitted by the tradition itself; it is a matter of individual choice.[37] "A fundamental challenge our civilization currently faces is to learn to live in the conditions of radical plurality. It is a challenge for politics, culture as well as religion."[38] We face an urgent need to speak and to think about Christian identity in new ways. Tomáš Halík suggests some ways forward in such dilemmas. We will focus on that in the third part of this chapter. Before that, we will describe the particular cultural context to which Halík is responding, i.e. the contemporary Czech culture.

BLESSED ARE THE DISTANT: CONTEMPORARY (CZECH) RELIGIOUS SCENE

Den Fremden verstehen – understanding the stranger is the hermeneutical principle of Halík's theology.[39] Halík believes that in order to understand Christian faith, a plurality of perspectives must be taken into consideration. Influenced by Nietzsche, he talks about perspectivism. This rather unusual philosophical stand-point, at least for a Catholic theologian, helps Halík to see theological and spiritual things from many different angles. On the results of such epistemology is Halík's emphasis on the category of patience. Faith and patience are sisters. Unfortunately, the Church often fails to recognize that and loses

---

[34] For example, John Milbank, "Postmodern Critical Augustinianism: A Short *Summa* in Forty Two Responses to Unasked Question," *Modern Theology* 7 (1991), pp. 225-237.

[35] According to Halík market economy and especially media have taken over the role of *religio* in the contemporary Western society: they make "big stories" and "celebrities", they are arbiters of truth, they interpret reality and define the importance of news.

[36] Cf. Livien Boeve, *Interrupting Tradition. An Essay on Christian Faith in a Postmodern Context* (Louvain: Peeters, 2003), pp. 79-80.

[37] Cf. Halík, "Globalizace a náboženství," p. 140.

[38] Halík, *Vzýván i nevzýván*, p. 128.

[39] We borrow the phrase Den Fremden verstehen from Theo Sundermeier, *Den Fremden verstehen: Eine praktische Hermeneutik* (Göttingen: Vandenhoeck & Ruprecht, 1996).

the opportunity to address those who are, for whatever reason, beyond its borders. This is, in Halík's opinion, what happened in the Czech Republic after the fall of communism.

Faith and Patience

Halík's interpretation of the current religious situation is indebted to Paul Tillich from whom he borrows the basic distinction between two groups of people. Tillich refuses a simple polar division between believers and unbelievers. He prefers to talk about the *open-minded* and *closed–minded* people. However, religion is not only the matter of cognitive abilities. Thus Halík shifts the intuition of the German theologian and suggests the differentiation between people of open *hearts* and those of close *hearts* (instead of minds). It is clear that Halík favours the former group over the latter. What does it mean to be open-minded? In Halík's opinion, it means to be opened to Mystery, to the Depth of Being that invites, and even excites the person to ask questions opening ways towards new interpretations of reality. This existential query is *faith*.[40]

Halík finds himself in full agreement with Gabriel Marcel: Mystery – contrary to a problem – cannot be conquered. "One must wait patiently at its threshold and persevere in it – must carry it in one's heart – just as Jesus's mother did."[41] In contrast, close-minded people do not hesitate to manipulate with reality.[42] They are ready to withdraw from questions which make their lives uneasy and perhaps uncomfortable. This is precisely what the Psalmist means, while he is crying: "They close their hearts to pity; with their mouths they speak arrogantly" (Ps 17:10).

Whether *I* consider *myself* to be open-minded or not, it is not important. According to the Christian confession of faith, God is not a God *of* Christians or *for* Christians. God is not a tribal deity, but the "Maker of heaven and earth" and the "Lord of history". God is always bigger – *Deus semper maior*. "God takes part in the story of *each* human being. God wants to enter the sanctuary of every human heart."[43] When

---

[40] The Czech language can't distinguish *faith* from *believe*. But in Halík's using of the Czech word for faith/believe ("víra") prevails the meaning of *faith* than *believe*.

[41] Halík, *Patience with God*, p. x.

[42] Jan Jandourek, *Tomáš Halík: Ptal jsem se cest* (Praha: Portál, 1997), p. 281.

[43] Halík, *Stromu zbývá naděje*, p. 81. Cf. Halík, *Divadlo pro anděly*, pp. 180-181.

explicit faith is not found there, God seeks an implicit one. Halík explains this idea with the help of Depth Psychology. Human psyche is like an iceberg – just one tenth of it is visible. This is what we call "consciousness". Nevertheless, it is only a minor part of the entire human psyche. This perspective analogously applies to religious faith. Halík claims that there are people who may refuse, for various reasons, to consider themselves to be believers in any traditional sense. However, in the hidden depth of their existence, their *hearts* "are fully open to Love".[44] "God speaks not only through His word but also through His silence. He speaks to people not only through His closeness, but also through His remoteness."[45] Open-minded people who are not explicit believers testify their implicit and anonymous faith through the acts of charity and their hope that life is a meaningful, although extremely difficult endeavour.[46]

These ideas might remind us of Karl Rahner and his concept of anonymous Christians. Halík's proposal, however, is based on a different ground. He has in mind an anonymous faith which, "*pours itself into love*"[47] or into hope.[48] Such an implicit faith includes a specific form of *patience*. This faith in a sense *is* patience. For patience is a metaphysical quality, an element engraved in being itself. Patience is a potential possibility of every person. Halík suggests that the patience of being – *passio essendi* – is prior to the drive to be – *conatus essendi*.[49] In other words, patience is an existential precondition of every action. Patience is something given to every conscious being. Everyone is free to refuse this gift and simply give up patience. But patience belongs to the wholeness of life and the fidelity to patience is already a participation in the splendour of being. It is really no accident that the translation of Halík's book *Vzdáleným na blízku* (literally: To Stand by the Distant) is aptly entitled *Patience with God*.

The category of patience reveals an enigmatic analogy between God and humanity. God can address us human beings implicitly,

---

[44] Halík, *Ptal jsem se cest*, p. 282.
[45] Halík, *Patience with God*, p. 211.
[46] Cf. Halík, *Patience with God*, pp. 197-198.
[47] Halík, *Stromu zbývá naděje*, p. 81.
[48] Halík, *Stromu zbývá naděje*, p. 82. Cf. the encyclical of Benedict XVI *Spe salvi* whose ideas Halík – not without reservations – develops. For the time that is beginning will be hope perhaps the most important. Cf. Tomáš Halík, *Dotkni se ran: Spiritualita nelhostejnosti* (Praha: Lidové noviny 2008), p. 239.
[49] This complex philosophical idea of *passio essendi* and *conatus essendi* is well captured by the Irish philosopher William Desmond, *God and the Between* (London: Wiley-Blackwell 2008).

somehow anonymously. We human beings can answer with equally implicit, anonymous faith which can be explained as patience of being. Despite the analogy there is of course no necessary direct proportion: An implicit action of God does not need to evoke implicit faith. People with open hearts wait for God as well as God waits for them. Both need patience.

An Impatient Faith – the Czech Situation

According to Halík, there is no real chasm between the religious situation in the Czech Republic and in other European countries. It is true though that the background of the Czech religious situation contains several specific elements. For example, in consequence of certain "historical injuries of the relationship between the nation and the Church" what emerged in Czech cultural history was a sort of anticlericalism, having the form of "love-hatred, an injured love that has developed into hatred."[50] It is necessary to take these wounds seriously otherwise they will continue to bleed. The only available treatment is to enhance *dialogue* between the Church and society. Nevertheless, the effort invested in such dialogue is hardly sufficient. Since the fall of the Iron Curtain, the Church repeats the same mistakes again and again. Sometimes naïvely, at some other times arrogantly, the Church tries to reconstruct the model of modern religiosity; i.e. a cultural religiosity without disturbing questions. Unfortunately, it completely overlooks the fact that religiosity has always existed also "at the periphery of the ecclesial religion and beyond its visible borders."[51] Moreover, this trend proves to be stronger and stronger. Enthusiasm for Christian values (especially for their moral and social aspects) has not vanished in the Czech society but "has just lost its traditional shape."[52] Greatest cultural heroes of Czech history (e.g. Bolzano, Havlíček, Palacký, Masaryk, Čapek, Patočka, Havel) were neither atheists, nor ordinary Church believers. In any case, a transcendent dimension of life, even though they had various names for it, was absolutely essential for them. Halík calls this phenomenon of the past and present *shy religiosity*: "as if the Czech believer felt on herself/himself a sceptical and ironic look of an unbeliever."[53]

Halík thus observes a gradual shift of Czech religiosity "from the surface inwards, from visible forms to informal forms, from

---

[50] Halík, "Katolická církev v České republice po roce 1989," p. 152.
[51] Halík, "Katolická církev v České republice po roce 1989," p. 152.
[52] Halík, "Katolická církev v České republice po roce 1989," pp. 152-153.
[53] Halík, "Katolická církev v České republice po roce 1989," p. 153.

metaphysical-theological vocabulary to the discourse of open humanism."[54] In sum, the highly secularized Czech culture is not irreligious or anti-religious but paradoxically quite open and sensitive to vertical-transcendent dimensions of human existence.

Among the factors that have contributed to this paradoxical state of affairs, we must also name the experience of totalitarianism. Communist totalitarianism functioned in a cunning way. Besides the external oppression using brutal force, which we would not wish to underestimate, the totalitarian regime preferred to target the internal side which made the situation even more serious.[55] Totalitarianism did not merely oppress, it ruined society and people from within. It easily happened that Christians and advocates of secular humanism found themselves on the same side of the battle field struggling for human rights.

Interestingly, the typically Czech shy religiosity gets out of its anonymity in dramatic moments of history. For example, after the Munich Treaty, which was an ante-room of totalitarianism in Central Europe, Czechs participated massively in several national pilgrimages with a clear religious and even Catholic character. The celebration of the 1100th anniversary of the death of St. Method the Apostle of Slavs, which happened still in the shadow of the Iron Curtain, was attended by 150.000 participants and thus it turned out to be the biggest post-war (religious) meeting in former communist Czechoslovakia. These and many other events attracted not only Christians but also a large crowd coming from beyond the official borders of the Church. Apart from such spontaneous and massive events numerous dissident activities were taking place in which secular and religious intellectuals from various ideological camps actively participated. Rather unlikely assemblies of activists such as Marxists, reform Communists, Conservative philosophers and Christians of all denominations were regularly working together and discussing thorny problems of politics, philosophy, and even religion. Without a common enemy; i.e. the totalitarian regime of the Communist party, however, these alliances of, in Halík's terms, "explicit believers and implicit believers" fades away.[56]

---

[54] Halík, "Katolická církev v České republice po roce 1989," p. 153.

[55] "Totalitarianism is never content to rule by external means, namely, through the state and a machinery of violence; thanks to its peculiar ideology..., totalitarianism has discovered a means of dominating and terrorizing human beings from within." Hannah Arendt, *The Origins of Totalitarianism* (New York: Harcourt Brace Jovanovich, 1973), p. 325.

[56] Cf. Halík, *Patience with God*, pp. 81-82.

Immediately after the fall of the totalitarian regime, the Church, and especially the Catholic Church, had a high degree of moral credibility in the Czech society. The Church was perceived as the only institution with authority.[57] Some ecclesial representatives were accepted almost uncritically. This was also the case with Tomáš Halík.[58] Regrettably, the Church began to be preoccupied with its own internal problems shortly afterwards. Probably the most serious one was the issue of incorporating the underground (dissident) Church into the official Church structures. What at first sight seemed to be a simple juridical problem opened a Pandora's box. The collaboration of many priests and religious people with the communist regime was discovered. This caused, on the one hand, a huge disappointment among intellectuals. On the other hand, a vast majority of people were simply perplexed about what was going on in the Church. At the end of the day, the interest in the Church decreased[59] and some obvious consequences appeared: "The Church has sunk into a tired pragmatism and has become one of the large badly functioning institutions. It has disappointed the Czech society, because it became clear that it differs from it little, therefore it has very little to offer."[60] The consequences are catastrophic. The crowds of religiously sensitive Czechs who just discovered their openness to spiritual questions, lost their patience overnight. The Czech Church could have been a pioneer in developing new ways in dealing

---

[57] The program "Desetiletí duchovní obnovy národa" ("A decade of a spiritual renewal of the nation") contributed to it. It was declared by Cardinal František Tomášek in November 1987. Tomáš Halík was one of the crucial figures of the program formation. But when he evaluates the result of the program, he is quite critical: "...I have a painful feeling at least in one respect: most of the priests and laymen grasped this project in a traditional sense as a succession of pilgrimages to national patrons and overlooked its very meaning – to show the Christian awareness of responsibility for the entire life of society." Halík, *Vzýván i nevzýván*, p. 208.

[58] The same can be said about Cardinal František Tomášek or the later auxiliary bishop of Prague Václav Malý.

[59] The collaboration of priests (grouped in societies such as "Peace Movement of the Catholic Clergy" and its "Pacem in terris"), and some laymen, with the communist regime has in fact been used as an instrument of enforced conformity of believers with the communist totalitarianism. This, in Halík's understanding, is one of paradoxes of Czech religious history. Cf. Libor Prudký, *Církve a sociální soudržnost v naší zemi* (Praha: UK FSV CESES, 2004), pp. 7-12; here p. 8. Available online: www.ceses.cuni.cz/CESES-20-version1-sesit04_10_prudky.pdf [accessed 12 January, 2014].

[60] Halík, *Vzýván i nevzýván*, p. 209.

wisely with secularization. The impatience of the Church leaders, however, buried this unique opportunity.

The Church failed not only in promoting dialogue but also in its public role in general. It is easier to care for a group of loyal members and occasionally moralize from the security of the Catholic fortress. Halík, together with a few other publicly involved Christians, repeatedly suggests that faith belongs to the public square in a different way. For Halík, the presence of the Church in the public domain does not mean any one-sided missionary strategy of recruiting souls. He rather sympathizes with Pope Benedict XVI who says that the Church should – in the manner of the Temple in Jerusalem – build a "courtyard for nations". This place would be intended for those who are not fully identified with the Church. It is not a coincidence that Benedict XVI formulated this request on his apostolic visit to the Czech Republic. Halík's vision goes even a step further and beyond the intention of Pope Benedict.

The metaphor used by the Pope contains residual traces of a triumphalist understanding of the Church (the Church as a "majestic building" that mercifully turns to "pagans"). Thus, Halík prefers to speak about the *mutual encounter of pilgrims* or *solidarity of pilgrims*. *Communio viatorum* presents the most fitting model of the Church.[61] Halík implements this ecclesiological model in the parish where he serves as the pastor of university students in the capital of the Czech Republic. The *phenomenon of Salvator*, as the citizens of Prague sometimes call Halík's parish, could be a theme of an extensive separate study. Here we limit ourselves to a short but unavoidable note. Halík's theology is inseparable from his praxis and vice-versa. Theological reflection of the necessarily dialogical nature of faith, of openness towards seekers, and of contemporary religious as well as social questions is not only an abstract theory. For Halík, this is above all a matter of praxis. And this praxis bears its fruits. In the course of the last 20 years, Halík baptized more than 1000 adult persons. The theological ideas which are behind Halík's pastoral success will be considered in what follows.

PATIENCE WITH GOD: AN ATTEMPT AT A THEOLOGY FOR A SECULAR AGE

Addressing Zacchaeus

---

[61] Halík, *Divadlo pro anděly*, p. 146.

Jesus of Nazareth approached people on the fringe of society without hesitation. Jesus was permanently seeking those who were "distant" and "habitually ascribed positive roles to scorned groups such as the Samaritans, detested customs officials, prostitutes and other sinners. He devoted Himself to lepers, the physically handicapped and others who were excluded from society."[62] Jesus, the master of paradox[63], blesses those *on the edge*. For him, the oppressed, the exploited, and the persecuted are in the centre. Nevertheless, there are not only socially excluded people but also those who are excluded spiritually. To use the current theological vocabulary we call them seekers.

For Halík, seekers are at the core of theology. The archetype of seekers is exemplified in the story of Zacchaeus (Luke 19:1–10). Zacchaeus' faith provides an adequate description of the religious situation in the West. Contemporary seekers seek deeper values then the consumerist mode of life is able to offer. They respect other people and are sensitive towards the mysterious *something* that transcends us, even though they do not have a name for this *something*. Their faith remains individual – not for their haughtiness but because they need to be free in their seeking. Seekers cannot stand the institutionalized spirituality because it often provides ready-made answers instead of momentous questions. Seekers accuse the Church of being too assured of itself. They detest ponderous hierarchical structures which do not allow space for individual opinions and responsibility. How often do we hear that the Catechism contains all we need to know about God? Or even worse, how often are sermons full of pathetic phrases such as: "Just believe, dear sister/brother, and everything will be better!"

When seekers are taken into consideration, then distinguishing between Church members and Churchless people is not really helpful anymore. A much clearer picture is achieved when we differentiate between engaged seekers and indifferent people. The current challenge for the Church is to develop strategies to address the former group and to attract the latter group. Unfortunately, the Church still prefers to address the flock of loyal members. In this respect, Halík suggests the following: "The future destiny of the Church and its position in [the Czech] society depends largely on whether it succeeds in 'calling Zacchaeuses' by name".[64]

---

[62] Halík, *Patience with God*, p. 13.

[63] Cf. Halík, *Patience with God*, p. 17.

[64] Tomáš Halík, "Oslovit vzdálené," *Universum* 4 (2007), pp. 17-20; here p. 17.

Halík, however, does not propose any kind of direct missionary activity. According to him, seekers-Zacchaeuses will never become standard parishioners. "Yes, generally speaking – and particularly if our Churches will appear in the future more or less the way they do now (and as far as I know, God has promised us no miracle in that respect) – the Zaccheuses will occupy a place on the fringe of the visible Church.... The point is that, without that 'fringe', the Church would not be a Church but a sect."[65] The Church needs seekers because a clear borderline between *members* and *outsiders* is a sign of a sect, not of a Church. What Halík actually suggests might be interpreted as analogous in a sense to Liberation theology because Halík proposes a recontextualized version of the preferential option for the poor. Following Jesus, the Church should see its calling to preferential option for the poor not just in the economic-social sense and should "*prefer people on the edge of the community of faith,*" people who remain somewhere "between religious certainty and atheism".[66] Zacchaeuses, the people on the fringe, can disturb the Church and individual Christians in their cosy religious dwelling. Seekers teach others that questions are sometimes more important than answers.

Halík reverses the order of things and says that the Church must learn from seekers instead of teaching them. He thus appears to be a postmodern thinker in his own way and presents his spiritual theology of interruption.[67] "Being able to take a look at how God appears from the standpoint of people who are searching, doubting, and questioning – isn't this a new, exciting, necessary and useful *religious experience?*"[68] Faith and doubt are actually not opposites but sisters; they need one another in order to balance their one-sidedness. Faith without doubt is blind, superficial and fanatic. Doubt without faith is cynical, sceptical and hopeless.[69] The dialogue between faith and doubt goes on in every

---

[65] Halík, *Patience with God*, p. 77.

[66] Halík, *Patience with God*, p. 16.

[67] The term interruption was developed by Johan Baptist Metz in the context of political theology. Johann B. Metz, *Glaube in Geschichte und Gesellschaft: Studien zu einer praktischen Fundamentaltheologie* (Mainz: Matthias Grünewald Verlag, 1977). Later, the Flemish theologian Lieven Boeve used the term in the context of fundamental theology, namely for conceptualizing dialogue between theology and postmodern philosophy. Lieven Boeve, *God Interrupts History: Theology in a Time of Upheaval* (New York: Continuum, 2007). Halík does not use this term but we believe it is appropriate to understand his theology in this way.

[68] Halík, *Patience with God*, p. 18.

[69] Cf. esp. Halík, *Co je bez chvění, není pevné*, pp. 40-45.

human mind. Every human being is *simul fidelis et infidelis*.[70] "It is necessary to preserve a *spirit of seeking*... it is necessary to *remain open* because only in that way may we reach the Kingdom of God."[71] The task of contemporary Christians is to become *seekers with seekers and ask questions*. Of course, there are also people among seekers who do not understand their seeking and questioning as a religious quest but as the search for truth, justice, and good. Then, there are also people who prefer to be quiet about their questions and doubts because they do not want to profane the marvel of seeking.

This original contribution to the current theological debate about the state of the Church in a secular age, which Halík offers, is based on his long-term engagement with the ambiguous phenomenon of atheism.

Taking Atheism Seriously

If faith is liberated from its certainties, the same must happen with atheism. The number of convinced atheists as well as convinced Christians and other dwellers is decreasing. Nevertheless, the enigmatic term *atheism* is still quite popular as self-identification. Many of those who declare their atheism actually refer to their religious indifference. This is usually connected with mistaken ideas about the Church, or sometimes it is caused by ignorance or simplistic images of god. This type of (un)faith might perhaps be called *apatheism*. Halík, however, focuses on a different type of atheism, which must be taken seriously. First of all, Halík provocatively challenges both Christians and atheists:

> Is atheism a sin? Yes – but only in the sense of a *debt*.... It is unfinished work, an unresolved matter, an uncompleted building. It is an unfinished and therefore unpalatable dish that needs a dash of the salt of faith. Atheism is a useful antithesis to naive, vulgar theism—but it is necessary to take a further step toward synthesis and mature belief.... But we must not fall prey to triumphalism or pride in these reflections—we must be aware that even 'mature belief' remains unfinished business as far as we are concerned and if we are to complete the task we need to take seriously the experience of atheism[.][72]

---

[70] Halík, *Chci, abys byl*, p. 20.
[71] Halík, *Patience with God*, p. 17. Cf. Halík, *Oslovit Zachea*, p. 10.
[72] Halík, *Patience with God*, 37.

Atheism is not only the opposite of belief. It is also a partner and even a teacher for those who believe. Atheism is "a mysterious contribution of historical time to the Easter drama."[73] Nevertheless, there is a wide variety of atheistic experiences: a "devil-may-care atheism"; a "forgetting God atheism" that substitutes God with godlings; a "proud atheism" claiming that God must not be; and last but not least, a "liberating atheism" which deconstructs false images of God and human projections of God. Atheism opens the way to the (re)discovery of the mystery (of God) again. Halík interprets this experience or attitude as *an atheism of passion* because of its genuine struggle with faith (in God).[74]

It is perhaps a provocative statement but, for Halík, a certain "logic of atheism" can be integrated into theology as a relevant methodological tool. Halík claims that there is a kind of religious experience common to atheists and believers, although both groups would interpret such experience differently.

Atheism in general insists that God is absent. Is this really an alien experience for Christians? If we think about the fundamental difference between God and the world, it seems reasonable to argue that "the divine way of being *present* [in the world] entails that we can experience God only as *absent*."[75] However, Halík dares to take one step further. The atheism of passion is a radical expression of "the death of faith on the cross of our world; the hour when the individual is plunged into inner and outer darkness, 'far from all suns'."[76] Halík claims that the story of Christianity and the story of the atheism of passion conflate in Jesus' scream: "My God, my God, why have you forsaken me?" (Mt 27:46; Mk 15:34) This atheism is a faith(less) confession of the truth of Good Friday. Thus, atheism is not necessarily a simple denial of God. It is, paradoxically, a sacramental experience. It is the very experience which Christians commemorate during the Good Friday liturgy and contemplate in the silent course of Holy Saturday. To be sure, Christians believe that this is not the end of Jesus' story. Indeed, *God alone has suffered the distance of God* but after the repose of Holy Saturday, faith which had to die on the cross and was buried, is *resurrected* and rises anew.[77] The atheism of passion brings into play an important message

---

[73] Halík, *Patience with God*, p. 43.

[74] Halík, *Patience with God*, pp. 40-41.

[75] Frederiek Depoortere, "Taking Atheism seriously: A Challenge for Theology in the 21st Century," in *Edward Schillebeeckx and Contemporary Theology*, F. Depoortere, L. Boeve and S. van Erp (eds.) (London, New York: T&T Clark, 2010), pp. 36-48.

[76] Halík, *Patience with God*, p. 41.

[77] Halík, *Patience with God,* p. 42.

for theology because it is, indeed, a genuine struggle with God who is silent, absent, and who seems to be dead.

The Church, in its teaching, is well-aware of the importance of this experience. The Pastoral Constitution on the Church in the Modern World *Gaudium et Spes* suggests that: "atheism must be accounted among the most serious problems of this age, and is deserving of closer examination."[78] However, Halík insists that it is necessary to exceed the horizon of Vatican II. Christian theology cannot afford to lose the (partial) truth of atheism. On the contrary, theology must ask the question: "Has not the time come to take into account the (partial) truth of atheism?"[79] But what is meant by this?

The Easter mystery reveals that the real enemy of faith is not atheism but *idolatry*. Halík reminds us that idolatry is not an ancient religious practice. Various forms of idolatry are present in contemporary context. Let us think about the so-called return of religion. Religiosity is returning, indeed. The question is: should the Church try to recognize the God of Jesus of Nazareth in contemporary religious trends? Should theology use the language of popular spirituality? Should Christians accept a sort of vague religiosity characterized by the popular phrase "I believe something must be above us?"[80] These questions would almost lead us to befriend (at least certain forms of) atheism. Why?

Hardly anybody takes God more seriously than real atheists.[81] That does not seem to be the case of contemporary spiritual movements in the West. Halík approaches fashionable spiritual streams with some suspicion. They characteristically neglect important moral topics in the name of superficial individualism. They sometimes do not really count on transcendence but rather promote a sort of inner spirituality of the self. Last but not least, this "returning religion" is in most cases afraid of *wounds* and covers them with precision. Everything must be fantastic, cool, amazing, and deeply felt. The modern "Religion within the Bounds of Bare Reason" (without dogmas) has turned into "Religion within the Bounds of Bare Experience" (without both dogmas and reason). Some people interpret this situation as a justification of fundamentalism that encourages a sort of return to faith without questions.[82] Especially

---

[78] *Gaudium et Spes*, no. 19.

[79] Halík, *Co je bez chvění*, p. 87.

[80] "Something-ism" is the most popular religious 'belief' among Czechs. "I do not believe in God, but there is certainly something above us," reads a common phrase.

[81] Cf. Halík, *Patience with God,* p. xii-xv.

[82] Halík, *Stromu zbývá naděje*, p. 83. Cf. Tomáš Halík, "Víra, rozum a hledání evropské identity," *Universum* 1 (2007), pp. 21-22.

extremely conservative forms of Christianity and Judaism focus almost exclusively on moral themes. However, their moral agenda is narrowed down to questions which obsessively revolve around sex, whereas crucial ethical problems (e.g. the developments of technology, media, environment, social responsibility) are usually neglected.[83] In Halík's opinion, this is "a clear hypocrisy, *exchange of moral for a moral indignation*.... It represents a big moral failure of contemporary Christianity."[84] Instead of proclaiming a living God, there is only the toxin of "moralin" (so Nietzsche) spread out by nowadays Pharisees. Nothing but idols.

Atheism is different and therefore valuable, Halík believes. Its main contribution to theology is its anti-idolatrous nature. Atheism functions as an interruption of belief. After all, the atheism of passion which is at the same time an atheism of pain wounded by the existence of evil in the world, presupposes faith in the good and right order of the world. Halík's bold statement that the paradox of God should be preached on the edges of faith and atheism[85] must be understood in this context. From the perspective of a theologian, an atheist represents the other who takes God seriously. Of course, not every atheist is like this. But those who are present a sufficient reason for enquiring into their experience, listening to their questions, and learning how they are seeking understanding.

Looking for the Altar of an Unknown God

Seeking out where we can meet God in today's world, we propose that it is in questioning. God is, indeed, in our questions. And Halík reminds us that: "There are questions that are so important that it is a pity to spoil them with answers."[86] Arguably, the question pertaining to God may be one of those best left unanswered. Thus, Halík suggests that one of the most appealing challenges for the Church in the 21st century is that of opening a new Areopag and of finding the altar of an unknown God.[87]

Paul preached the Gospel of an unknown God in Athens (Acts 17, 22-34). Theologians are called to follow Apostle Paul in this courageous task. For, indeed, the current state of affairs resembles the situation of those who were listening to Paul on Mount Areopag. God is no longer

---

[83] Halík, *Stromu zbývá naděje*, p. 54.
[84] Halík, *Stromu zbývá naděje*, p. 55.
[85] Cf. Halík, *Patience with God*, p. 108.
[86] Halík, *Chci, abys byl*, p. 15.
[87] Cf. Halík, *Patience with God*, pp. 113-121.

well-known. It is rather the case that the God of Jesus of Nazareth has ceased to be self-evident. The God of the Christian faith has become a sort of stranger.

What is behind this alienation? What if the decline of Christianity in the postmodern context is not caused by atheism or agnosticism? What if Christian faith is disappearing because our (Western) world is full of additional gods? Have we ever considered the idea that the God of the Gospels was not replaced by disbelief but by different beliefs? When this perspective is applied, it seems that there is a multitude of gods. All are easily available. All are moreover *very-well known* gods. These gods and their cults usually offer answers and solutions which Christian theology is not able to give. Maybe theology is guilty in this respect. But its guilt does not lie in refusing to answer. Theology is guilty because it does not ask enough questions.

The unknown God of paradox, preached by Paul on Areopag, has too often been substituted by some known god. Indeed, theologians struggle with an omnipresent temptation to treat God in human, *all too human* terms. The temptation to swap the paradoxical God of Jesus of Nazareth for some kind of a harmonized being accessible to our knowledge without disturbance or questions is something that runs through the course of Christian history. Nicholas Lash observes that theological questioning as a search for understanding has been replaced by the explanatory discourse. However, "explanation, unlike understanding, if successful comes to an end."[88] Theology seems to be more or less unable to deal with the paradox that God dwells in the question. What would be the consequences of Halík's call to set up the altar of an unknown God again? Let us speculate for a moment.

First, we have to go back to modernity and reinterpret the story of reason. Modernity changed the paradigm of thinking. The modern ethos was constituted by such claims as (i) the supreme authority of reason (*ratio*), (ii) the highest authority of natural sciences, especially mathematics and (iii) the idea of eternal progress.[89] Above all, modernity brought about changes in the conception of knowledge. For the first time, knowledge was defined as power (Bacon). Knowledge made humans effective and only what was effective was deemed knowledge. Thus, knowledge enabled humans to become masters of the universe (Descartes).[90]

---

[88] Nicholas Lash, *Holiness, Speech and Silence: Reflections on the Question of God* (Aldershot, Burlington, VT: Ashgate Pub., 2004), pp. 1-22.

[89] Cf. Robert B. Pippin, *Modernism as a Philosophical Problem: On the Dissatisfaction of European High Culture* (Oxford: Blackwell, 1991), p. 4.

[90] Cf. Jan Patočka, *Heretical Essays in the Philosophy of History*

Naturally, this modern shift changed theology and heavily influenced theological epistemology. The idea that humans could speak clearly about the universe and master it led to the conviction that the same humans could speak clearly about God. In short, modernity developed a new form of rationalism, the rationalism of mastery[91] and theologians used this mastery to conquer the altar of an unknown mysterious God. The question of God was replaced by the problem of God.[92] In other words, theologians sought an unequivocal, clear and distinct language. And this is, more or less, our own conviction. Theology should adopt an unequivocal language in order to argue in the public square, to be perfectly understandable for ordinary people, and thus to attract them to Churches. According to these principles, which are rather the principles of early modern science,[93] God was perceived as an object. The result was the univocalisation of God and a shift from the question of God to answers about God.

Postmodern criticism proclaims the end of clear and distinct ideas, formulated from the bird's perspective, about the world, human beings and, last but not least, God. Postmodern critical consciousness initiates a different strategy, namely a sensitivity for the inexpressible, for the unrepresentable and for otherness. To use technical theological vocabulary; postmodernity takes *mystery* seriously again.

Halík works with a sort of postmodern critique as well. Remember that he went through the experience of totalitarianism. After the hell of totalitarian oppression, no one can claim that God is easily at our disposal. On the contrary, Halík's post-totalitarian perspective suggests that, when faced with the question of God, we must begin from the viewpoint of the night, darkness and uncertainty. Thus, the fact that God becomes a sort of a stranger is not necessarily an impasse. The current crisis is not a threat. Rather it is an opportunity to open up new

---

(Chicago: Open Court, 1996), pp. 83-84.

[91] Cf. Patočka, *Heretical Essays*, p. 110.

[92] Gabriel Marcel makes a famous distinction between *problem* and *mystère*. "A problem is something which I meet, which I find completely before me, but which I can therefore lay siege to and reduce. But a mystery is something in which I am myself involved, and it can therefore only be thought of as a sphere where the distinction between what is in me and what is before me loses its meaning and initial validity." Gabriel Marcel, *Being and Having* (Westminster: Dacre Press, 1949), p. 117.

[93] It must be noted that these principles we describe in the body of text are not identical with the principles of late modern science as shows, for example, Werner Heisenberg, *Physics and beyond: Encounter and Conversations* (New York: Harper and Row, 1971).

ways of understanding God and interpreting the role of Christianity in the world. Halík thus suggests a sort of recontextualizing of the idea of medieval university in order to enhance contextually plausible and theologically valid thought in the current secularized context.

The Church as a School/University

The idea of a university is grounded in service to wisdom. Halík believes that instead of the modern *sola ratione*, the path of wisdom as *docta ignorantia* must be promoted. According to Halík, spreading wisdom or rather spreading an educated faith is the most appealing task of the Church in the postmodern context. An intelligent faith does not fear doubts and can cope with God the stranger; *Deus semper maior*. Through this lens, Halík interprets the call for New Evangelization.

Halík does not understand "The New Evangelization" proposed by John Paul II., as a triumphalist religious mobilization. Were the call for Evangelization to be understood in that way, it is destined for failure. The New Evangelization should be a humble and patient 'return to the school.'[94] It is "a challenge for a really *new*, even though quieter, slower, but first and foremost, *deeper* introduction of the therapeutic power of the Gospel to the very heart of our culture, and also to its hidden places."[95] Christianity as *religio*, as the "sacred canopy" of the Western culture is gone. For long centuries Christianity was so present in European society that it became too self-evident and the mystery of God was forgotten. A continuing *metanoia*, as the core of faith, was slowly disappearing.[96] This school, however, is not the indoctrination of pupils by masters. It is rather the community of students (seekers of wisdom) and teachers who have already learnt that silence is the only possible answer to certain questions. This school is a community of shared life and sharing knowledge and prayer.

Halík reminds his readers of Rahner's dictum – with which he agrees – that Christianity of the third millennium will be either mystical or it will not be at all. Nonetheless, Halík adds that Christian faith of the 21st century must also be a meditative-reflective faith. It is important to mention that in this respect Halík finds a strong ally in another German theologian – Joseph Ratzinger/Benedict XVI.

Pope Benedict XVI once said that the Church should be rather a creative minority instead of a mass organization. Halík expresses a similar idea in the form of irony: "I do not really understand who has

---

[94] Halík, *Stromu zbývá naděje*, 70.
[95] Halík, *Dotkni se ran*, 74.
[96] Halík, *Dotkni se ran*, 75.

come up with the idea that Christianity is for masses." All this is in line with Halík's call for a *deep theological and spiritual renewal* in order to present Christianity as a "lifestyle".[97] This ought to be the "Christianity of the second breath" based only on faith, hope, love – and their *school*.[98] "Maybe in the Czech Republic, where classical forms of the Church and religion were so strongly devastated and deracinated, this new form of Christianity is more likely to be successful than anywhere else where the end of the old form of religion is not as apparent yet."[99] Maybe this is true for the entire Europe.

CONCLUSION

In what has been said so far we tried to demonstrate that the theological enterprise of Tomáš Halík is extensive. Halík discusses a wide range of themes, questions and theological problems. He proposes various original ideas. What we have learned from Halík can be summarized in four points. Firstly, the current historical form of Christianity is in crisis, a crisis caused by secularization. Halík insists that secularization of Western societies is not a threat. For him, this crisis is an opportunity, knocking on the door of Christianity. This crisis should be seen as the ongoing development of Christian tradition. Secondly, in order to deal with the current state of affairs we must engage in an open dialogue. This dialogue includes serious engagement with secularized society and contemporary philosophy. According to Halík, the Church has to give up its closed mentality, the mentality of a religious ghetto. Consequently, Christian theology and the Church must welcome 'critical friends'. Atheism is not the enemy. Seekers are brothers and sisters. Certain forms of atheism and their respective criticism of religion challenge the Christian tradition to be more authentic. Certain experiences of seeking God, asking questions and looking for real depth should be incorporated into the life of the Church. Thirdly, this requires the virtue of courage. The task of the Church is to deconstruct its borders instead of constructing high walls. Halík emphasizes that the Church must welcome people who stand on the edges. The Church is compelled to meet these edge dwellers, many of whom show an interest in religion and Church related affairs but they, like Zacchaeus, need to be encouraged to meet with Jesus in *their* houses. Likewise, Halík suggests a broader ecclesial concept as a model for the Church in the postmodern context. Fourthly, Halík does not

---

[97] Halík, *Night of the Confessor*, pp. 126-127.
[98] Halík, *Night of the Confessor*, pp. 112-113.
[99] Halík, *Chci, abys byl*, p. 10.

propose any easy solution for the current crisis of Christianity and its ecclesial forms. He insists that we must live creatively throughout this crisis, and that the crisis is essential for the well-being of Christianity. The experience of crisis is an essential part of Christian faith.

These lessons gained from Halík lead us to the following critical questions. Firstly, we are convinced that we have to think about God in a different way. Halík's presentation of an open image of God is appealing. Instead of the closed images of *a too well known God*, it is essential to consider the concepts of *an unknown God*, and of *God the stranger*. However, we suspect that Halík uses the aforementioned terms describing God's mystery somehow automatically. God's mystery, indeed, exceeds our theological mastery; i.e. the knowledge of God we obtained through the gift of revelation. The very fact that we call God *an ultimate mystery*, or *the depth of our existence* is, in one way or another, a part of our knowledge of God. Thus we find a lack of more precise distinction between mystery and revelation in Halík's works. Let us illustrate this critical point with the following example. Halík claims that atheists contradict their own atheism when they fight against evil in this world. The struggle for the good and justice, in Halík's opinion, presupposes a sort of belief in some guarantor of a meaningful order in the world.[100] It seems that Halík operates here with a *known God*, at least, with a God which is known to him. The question is: How can Halík make such an easy link between God and the meaningful order of reality and, at the same time, claim that God is *an unknown mystery*? Thus, it seems that, for Halík, the concept of an unknown God belongs to the order of "known knows" about God. Of course, this is a legitimate position, however, Halík's readers would probably expect a more precise elaboration what these "known knows" about God contain. In other words, Halík's fundamental theological opinion: "God is mystery – that should be the first and last sentence of any theology;"[101] should be complemented with the confession, *but still he has become a man.*

Secondly, Halík challenges the classical distinction between believers and unbelievers and replaces it with new counter-poles: open-minded people and close-minded people. As long as Halík uses this new concept as a descriptive tool, and we believe he does, everything is all-right. If the description turns out to be a judgement, we have a problem. In some texts, Halík seems to be dangerously close to a God-like-position when locating people in the aforementioned groups. It has to be added that we believe that when we consider what Halík says about

---

[100] Cf. Halík, *Stromu zbývá naděje,* p. 189.
[101] Halík, *Patience with God,* p. 46.

open-minded and close-minded people within the entire context of his thought this concern proves to be pointless. Nevertheless, we have a second, more serious difficulty in this respect. Halík's distinction between the open-minded ones and close-minded ones together with his emphasis on the Church as the school of wisdom results in identifying all (good) Christians as ruminative. Not all Christians are sophisticated intellectuals.

This is linked to our third critical point. Halík certainly favours an open attitude towards culture. Thus, he stays close to the so-called correlation theology which postulates a sort of continuity between Christianity and the world. This becomes clear when Halík's analysis of secularization is taken into account. Accoridng to Halík, secularization is a Christian by-product. The correlationist orientation is also visible in other fields of Halík's interest; e.g. interreligious dialogue; the engagement with non-Christian prayer-techniques, etc. He prefers similarities over differences, continuity over discontinuity. Halík stands in line with important theological figures such as Paul Tillich, Edward Schillebeeckx, or Nicholas Lash etc. A potential danger in this line of theological thinking is reductionism of the genuine otherness of the other, despite explicit proclamations that otherness must be respected and approached with humility in dialogue. The emphasis on one-sided continuity between different experiences (both religious and secular) may result in projecting our Christian image on the *Other*.

To be sure, Halík balances his correlationist position with reference to postmodern hermeneutical philosophy, especially to such thinkers as Gianni Vattimo and Richard Kearney. Postmodern hermeneutics is very sensitive with regard to the particularity of the other. Only if we respect the particularity of others, can we claim the right to be respected in our own particularity. We can also put it vice-versa. Only if we are explicit about our own particularity; i.e. if we do not feel embarrassed for differences and discontinuity in relation to others, are we able to respect the others in their genuine otherness. We believe that Halík's turn towards postmodern philosophy of religion is a movement in the right direction. We await with much enthusiasm Halík's new project bearing the working-title *the afternoon of faith* – a sort of *post-faith*. We dare to say, however, that it will certainly be a valuable theological-philosophical contribution, if Halík remains himself – an author who goes beyond the borders of theology, philosophy and sociology. Halík's work is neither systematic theology, nor mere spirituality and by no means a sort of relativistic philosophy of religion. The entire project of Halík's intellectual and public work intertwines a radical hermeneutical (postmodern) position with traditional standpoints. This results in his attempt to overcome the modern division between theology and philosophy by focusing on *wisdom*. Thus, we suggest that the *afternoon of faith* should not be a repetition of previous ideas but a new synthesis based on further research in biblical studies, systematic theology, sociology of religion, and postmodern philosophy. Halík must retain his identity of an essayist and should enlarge his identity as a philosopher. If that happens we will find in his forthcoming works a dossier for Christianity in the postmodern cultural context. Tomáš Halík must remain (as he has always been) standing between and reminding us of paradoxes.

BIBLIOGRAPHY

Arendt, Hannah. 1973. *The Origins of Totalitarianism*. New York: Harcourt Brace Jovanovich.
Berger, Peter L. 1992. *A Far Glory: The Quest for Faith in an Age of Credulity*. New York: Free Press.
Berger, Peter L. and Luckmann, Thomas. 1971. *The Social Construction of Reality: A Treatise in the Sociology of Knowledge*. Harmondsworth: Penguin Books.
Boeve, Lieven. 2007. *God Interrupts History: Theology in a Time of Upheaval*. New York: Continuum.
Boeve, Livien. 2003. *Interrupting Tradition. An Essay on Christian Faith in a Postmodern Context*. Louvain: Peeters.
Depoortere, Frederiek. 2010. "Taking Atheism seriously: A Challenge for Theology in the 21st Century," in *Edward Schillebeeckx and Contemporary Theology*, F. Depoortere, L. Boeve and S. van Erp (eds.), London/New York: T & T Clark, 2010), 36-48.
Desmond, William. 2008. *God and the Between*. London: Wiley-Blackwell.
Gogarten, Friedrich. 1953. *Verhängnis und Hoffnung der Neuzeit. Die Säkularisierung als theologisches Problem*. Stuttgart: Friedrich Vorwerk.
Halík, Tomáš. 2000. "Katolická církev v České republice po roce 1989," in *Společnost v přerodu*. Praha: Masarykův ústav AV ČR, 2000.
Halík, Tomáš. 2002. *Co je bez chvění, není pevné*. Praha: Lidové noviny.
Halík, Tomáš. 2003. "Globalizace a náboženství," in *Globalizace*, Václav Mezřický (ed.), Praha: Portál.
Halík, Tomáš. 2004. *Vzýván i nevzýván*. Praha: Lidové noviny.
Halík, Tomáš. 2007. "Oslovit vzdálené," *Universum*. Vol. 17. No. 4, 17-20.
Halík, Tomáš. 2007. "Víra, rozum a hledání evropské identity." *Universum*. Vol. 17. No. 1, 21-22.
Halík, Tomáš. 2008. *Dotkni se ran: Spiritualita nelhostejnosti*. Praha: Lidové noviny.

Halík, Tomáš. 2009. *Patience with God: The Story of Zaccheus Continuing in Us*. New York: Doubleday.
Halík, Tomáš. 2009. *Stromu zbývá naděje: Krize jako šance*. Praha: Lidové noviny.
Halík, Tomáš. 2010. *Divadlo pro anděly: Život jako náboženský experiment*. Praha: Lidové noviny.
Halík, Tomáš. 2012. *Chci, abys byl. Křesťanství po náboženství*. Praha: Lidové noviny.
Halík, Tomáš. 2012. *Night of the Confessor: Christian Faith in an Age of Uncertainty*. New York: Image Books – Doubleday.
Halík, Tomáš. 2013. "Křesťanství a laicita." *Universum*. Vol. 23. No. 1, 17-19.
Heisenberg, Werner. 1971. *Physics and beyond: Encounter and Conversations*. New York: Harper and Row.
Jandourek, Jan. 1997. *Tomáš Halík: Ptal jsem se cest*. Praha: Portál.
Kovář, M. "Biskup Edna a Jan Nep. Brynych." *Sborník historického kroužku*. Vol. 4. No. 1, 1-3.
Lash, Nicholas. 2004. *Holiness, Speech and Silence: Reflections on the Question of God*. Aldershot, Burlington, VT: Ashgate Pub.
Luckmann, Thomas. 1967. *The invisible Religion: The Problem of Religion in Modern Society*. New York: Maxmillan.
Marcel, Gabriel. 1949. *Being and Having*. Westminster: Dacre Press.
Metz, Johann B. 1977. *Glaube in Geschichte und Gesellschaft: Studien zu einer praktischen Fundamentaltheologie*. Mainz: Matthias Grünewald Verlag.
Milbank, John. 1991. "Postmodern Critical Augustinianism: A Short *Summa* in Forty Two Responses to Unasked Question," *Modern Theology*. No. 7, 225-237.
Patočka, Jan. 1996. *Heretical Essays in the Philosophy of History*. Chicago: Open Court.
Pippin, Robert B. 1991. *Modernism as a Philosophical Problem: On the Dissatisfaction of European High Culture* (Oxford: Blackwell,), p. 4.
Prudký, Libor. 2004. *Církve a sociální soudržnost v naší zemi*, Praha: UK FSV CESES, 2004.
Schleiermacher, Friedrich D. E. 1999 [1799]. *Über die Religion: Reden an die Gebildeten unter ihren Verächtern*. G. Meckenstock (ed.), Berlin/New York: de Gruyter.
Sundermeier, Theo. 1996. *Den Fremden verstehen: Eine praktische Hermeneutik*. Göttingen: Vandenhoeck & Ruprecht.
Taylor, Charles. 2007. *A Secular Age*. Cambridge, MT: Harvard University Press.
Wallace, Anthony F. C. 1966. *Religion: An Anthropological View*. New York: Random House.

CHAPTER VII

CHURCH FOR THE SEEKERS

TOMÁŠ HALÍK

If we want to understand the spiritual situation of contemporary Western postsecular society we have to move from the traditional believers-nonbelievers paradigm to the new *seekers-dwellers paradigm*.

Believers and nonbelievers are not two strictly separated groups. The contemporary Western person is often "*simul fidelis et infidelis*".

The number of *dwellers* – traditional believers who fully identify themselves with the teaching and practice of institutional Church – is decreasing. Traditional religiosity is losing its "socio-cultural biosphere". Also among Church-goers we find many *seekers*, who are loyal Church members though not completely satisfied with its contemporary form and fashion. Their faith is not a treasure of certainties for them, but a journey, a way of seeking, a way into the depths of meaning.

On the other hand the number of *convinced atheists* is also slowly decreasing.

Among those who *call themselves atheists*, we can find many agnostics, some "apatheists' and "religious analphabets" (those who are indifferent towards religion). We also find some radical opponents and critics of the contemporary Church, but a growing group of those who occasionally identify themselves as atheists should more adequately be called *seekers* – those who are attracted by various kinds of new spiritual options such as westernized versions of Eastern religions or esoteric spirituality. In the Czech Republic, many of those who would call themselves "spiritual but not religious" in Western countries, spontaneously and without much reflection call themselves "atheists", because (besides other things) to be an atheist is considered normal (and to be a believer means to be an odd person and a member of a marginal minority). "To be an atheist" means often in fact just "to keep distance from the Church".

The indefinite and ambiguous "grey zone" between traditional believers and convinced atheists is growing. This "grey zone" is in fact very diverse and multifarious.

I am deeply convinced that the future of the Church depends mainly on her ability to communicate with "seekers".

Those who focus on traditional believers and Church-goers tend to conclude that a society, where the number of people who identify themselves with the Church is decreasing, is therefore becoming atheistic. But this erroneous conclusion is based on understanding believers as "dwellers" (those who identify themselves with the current form of the Church or with the sort of Church doctrine to which they have been exposed and internalized or which they consider to be the official teaching).

This situation can be clearly illustrated by the example of the Czech Republic. Czech society is considered to be one of the most atheist societies in the European Union, if not on the entire planet. This evaluation is based primarily on the regular census and on various investigations into public opinion. More methodologically appropriate research projects show that religious diversity in the Czech society is much wider than what the popular stereotype about Czech atheism would suggest.

It was already Saint Augustine who insisted that "many who think they are outside are in fact inside and many of those who think they are inside are in fact outside". Indeed, among seekers who are outside the borders of institutionalized Church we would find many deeply religious and spiritual people.

On the other hand we can take for granted that among those who formally claim their adherence to the Church and who regularly or occasionally attend Church services, there is a large number of people who only partially identify with the contemporary shape of the Church (its institutional and doctrinal form).

Many Church representatives would perhaps be surprised by the difference between what a large number of "practising Catholics" believe about God, afterlife and many other aspects of faith and the official teaching of the Church, and also by the percentage of Catholics who actually do follow the guidelines of Catholic sexual ethics, especially in the area of premarital sex and contraception.

In many countries, especially in Western Europe many people have left the Catholic Church during the last several decades and consider themselves to be "ex-Catholics". In the Czech Republic, undoubtedly also because there is no obligatory "Church tax", cases of formal leaving the Church are relatively few. Many of those who gave up on the Church in its contemporary shape inwardly do not feel the need to express it officially.

Those who are only "partially identified" we find on both ends of the spectrum: among "progressivists" who think the Church has left the direction of Vatican Council II, and also among "conservatives" and "traditionalists", who think that the Church has gone too far – during Vatican II and in the following decades – in opening itself towards the contemporary world. It seems that when Church representatives think about these "partially identified" and about "ex-Catholics", they primarily ask the question how to bring them back into the current ecclesial fold. It is of course very desirable if the bishops enter dialogue with the critics of the Church about their objections and complaints concerning its contemporary shape. But maybe a real pastoral responsibility should lead to a deeper reflection: Could the actual disagreements on particular issues be just substitute problems? Could the real question lie on a deeper level? Are those who criticize the Church today interested just in solving the several particular problems to which they are pointing? Of course, no specific problems of the Church should be taboo. But maybe the real source of so much dissatisfaction with Church today is the desire of at least some contemporary people for such forms of religious life for which the "static religion" of dwellers opens no space.

If that is the case, it implies that as the Church is looking for a satisfactory response to the problem of "partial identification" and to the fact that a growing number of people are leaving the Church, it cannot just struggle with how to fix particular problems and respond to particular complaints and requirements of those who are dissatisfied. It has to rethink and redefine theologically its very essence and calling (and consequently implement that calling in pastoral, teaching, prophetic and humanitarian ministry).

The question we are facing is this: Should the Church function as a comfortable home for dwellers or should it also become an open space for seekers? Should its solidarity with people of our time, which the Church promised in the opening sentence of the constitution *Gaudium et spes*, imply not only that it will be "crying with those who are crying and rejoicing with those who are rejoicing" but also seeking with those who are seeking?

***

A significant step towards a more open attitude of the Church in relation to the seekers has been the new understanding of laity (*laicité*), secular humanism and modern atheism in the documents of the Vatican Council II. It seemed that the Vatican II may lead to *a transition from Catholicism to catholicity,* a transition from Catholicism as a counter-culture against modernity towards an open-minded Christianity understood in an ecumenical and dynamic way (the Church as God's people on its pilgrimage through history).

But the five decades that have passed after the reformist council have been filled with polemics among various interpreters of that council, polemics between the proponents of "hermeneutics of continuity" on the one hand, insisting on the letter of the documents and warning against too radical innovations in theology and pastoral care, and on the other hand the proponents of "hermeneutics of discontinuity", who in the name of "the spirit of the council" understood that council as the first step in a direction, which has to lead towards further reforms. An ambivalent relationship to the legacy of the council is clearly evidenced also in the thinking of Joseph Ratzinger – Benedict XVI.

On the one hand in Ratzinger's thinking (after a certain conservative turn caused especially by his encounter with the "cultural revolution" at Western universities in the late sixties and also by the turbulences in the Church after the Vatican II) we find a particular critical attitude towards numerous features of modern civilisation, and an awareness of the danger hidden in the attempts to bring the modern process of human emancipation to an extreme, namely to the secularist denial of any transcendent dimension of human being and culture.

On the other hand – especially in the later years of his pontificate – this Pope – theologian writes and speaks about a "healthy laicity", and says how irresponsible and tragic it would be to try to move the Church and society in some kind of nostalgia back into the premodern period and to overlook the immeasurable positive results brought about by the Enlightenment, modernity, scientific rationality and the separation of religion and political power.

Joseph Ratzinger took seriously the important revisions of the nature of Enlightenment, proposed by a number of contemporary thinkers (many of them originally influenced by Marxism), as they became aware of the "dialectics of the Enlightenment" and many *aporias* of modernity. His famous dialogue with the leftist philosopher Jürgen Habermas on the ground of the Catholic Academy in Munich shortly before the beginning of his pontificate culminated in a mutual agreement, that Christianity and secular humanism need each other, in order to correct or balance each other's onesidedness.[1] Similarly, before the British Parliament in September 2010, Pope Benedict said that the world of secular rationality and the world of religious faith need each other and should not be afraid to enter a deep and continuing dialogue for the good of our civilisation.

The strong emphasis he puts on the role of reason and rationality has been a lasting feature of Ratzinger's thought. We can just mention his repeated call for a strong bond between faith and reason and a "new alliance between faith and science". Ratzinger always sharply opposed religious fanaticism and fundamentalism, and also fantasizing mysticism and irrationalism both in "new religious movements" and in postmodern relativism. But he also criticized the modernist tendency to reduce

---

[1] Cf. Jürgen Habermas and Joseph Ratzinger, *The Dialectics of Secularization: On Reason and Religion* (San Francisco: Ignatius Press 2006).

rationality only to empirically measurable facts, he emphasized that he defends "an open rationality, not a closed one".

In his view reason and faith can develop their greatest potential only in mutual dialogue, faith without thinking and reason without moral and spiritual dimensions of faith can both be extremely dangerous. The dialogue between reason and faith was for him a *necessary foundation for interreligious dialogue*. According to Ratzinger the coalition of reason and faith leads to tolerance and protects religion from fanaticism and connecting religious faith with violence.

Pope Benedict always defended the classical connection of faith and (metaphysical) reason, Logos, as understood in Greek philosophical tradition, and he refused to see this connection as a historical coincidence. It seemed that for Ratzinger the marriage between Christian theology and classical metaphysics is indissoluble.

This is why so many were surprised to hear Ratzinger's "invitation for agnostics" not to be too much concerned by the fact that for them God is rather an "unknown God", surrounded by impenetrable mystery, but rather to dare entering the adventure of "faith as an experiment", to risk counting on "God as a hypothesis". In his speech in Subiaco immediately before the death of his predecessor cardinal Ratzinger offered to "our non-believing friends" an interesting suggestion: modern science taught us to operate with the hypothesis of "methodological atheism", to think "as if there was no God" (*etsi Deus non daretur*). But shouldn't we all today – in the area of ethics – including those, who "cannot find any way of accepting God", live, behave and decide "as if there was God", *velutisi Deus daretur*?

Several years later this Pope offered agnostics another interesting suggestion: he proposed – during his visit in the Czech Republic in September 2009 – the idea of the "courtyard for the nations": the Church should – similarly as the Jews in the Temple of Jerusalem – offer certain space for those who do not fully share its faith.

The Church, if it wants to avoid the tendency of becoming an elitist sect, must not care just for those "fully identified", but it should open space also for those who do not fully share Christian faith, for seekers. The idea that the Church needs to be in touch with people who believe in an "unknown God" or who just vaguely desire for "something beyond", is very important. Yet it is not easy to resist the suspicion that behind the metaphor of the "courtyard of nations" there still operates a certain triumphalist understanding of the Church. Is the Church today really in the position to open the "courtyard for gentiles" or is she rather sent out to humbly look for various "gentile courtyards" and to try there to address the gentiles in their own language as for example Paul did on the Areopag? Are we not in a situation today where all that remains of the once glorious temple-like form of Christian religion is nothing more but the Veiling wall?

***

A certain answer to these questions can be found in the new understanding of the Church as presented by Pope Francis. Before the beginning of the conclave, which followed after Pope Benedict's resignation, the Argentinian cardinal Bergolio quoted the famous passage from the New Testament: Jesus stands at the door and knocks. And Bergolio added: Jesus today knocks on the other side of the door. He stands inside and wants to go out of the Church.

The Church, as Pope Francis keeps reminding us, has to go out, it has to leave the safe spaces in which it used to stay. It should operate as a field hospital, to be always present especially in places where people suffer and where it is necessary to bind wounds.

In my book *Touch the Wounds*[2] I expressed my deep conviction: A religion that ignores people's misfortune and suffering is an opium of the people. Crucial to my Christian faith is one particular scene in John's Gospel – the encounter between the apostle Thomas and the resurrected Christ. Within Thomas' heart, as in the hearts and minds of many people today, faith and doubt are in conflict. Only when Jesus shows him His wounds does Thomas cry out: My Lord and my God!

Our world is full of wounds. It is my conviction that those who close their eyes to the wounds in our world have no right to say: My Lord and my God. A God that does not bear wounds is a dead God. When someone offers me their God, I ask: Is it the God of love, wounded by our world's suffering? I am not willing to believe in any other god.

I once commented ironically on the famous legend that aptly symbolises the beginnings of "imperial Christianity" (Christendom), the story of the Emperor Constantine's dream. In his dream Constantine saw a cross and heard the words: "Conquer with this". Next morning he fixed crosses to the standards of his troops and won the battle. I wondered how the history of Europe and the history of the Church would have turned out if the emperor had interpreted his dream rather more intelligently.

Today we all stand before the cross as before a dilemma. Will the cross be for us a battle standard, a nostalgic memorial to the time when it was a sign of triumphalism and power? Or will we grasp the *kenotic* message of the cross: the man Jesus, although he was God's equal,

---

[2] Cf. Tomáš Halík, *Dotkni se ran* (Praha: Nakl. Lidové noviny, 2008).

emptied himself and became as one of the people and took upon himself the form of a servant.

If we wish to follow Christ, we must abandon any yearning after a privileged place in this world. Each of us must become "one of the people", and take seriously that solidarity with the people of our time, to which the Church committed itself in the beautiful words at the beginning of the pastoral constitution "*Gaudium et spes*".

Let us not fear that we would thereby lose ourselves in the crowd and lose our Christian identity. What will distinguish us from the mass of people around us (but what will unite us at the same time with those with whom we ourselves would not seek an alliance), will not be the crosses on our banners, but instead the willingness to "take upon ourselves the form of a servant." This life orientation of kenosis, self-surrender, means, within a civilisation oriented mainly towards material success, a conspicuously non-conformist attitude. Those who live this way can be a hidden "salt of the earth" and also a highly visible "light of the world".

BIBLIOGRAPHY

Habermas, Jürgen and Ratzinger, Joseph. 2006. *The Dialectics of Secularization: On Reason and Religion*. San Francisco: Ignatius Press.

Halík, Tomáš. 2008. *Dotkni se ran*. Praha: Nakl. Lidové noviny.

ABOUT THE AUTHORS

Tomáš Halík PhD, DD (born 1948) graduated from Charles University, Prague, in philosophy, sociology and psychology. He studied theology in secret courses in Prague and at post-graduate level in Rome and Wroclaw after 1989. In 1978 he was secretly ordained a priest at Erfurt (GDR) and for the next 11 years was active in the "underground Church" and as a close colleague of Cardinal Tomasek. After 1989 he became the first secretary of the Czech Bishops' Conference and consultant to the Pontifical Council for dialogue with non-believers (1990-93). He is currently Professor of the Philosophy and Sociology of Religion at the Philosophical Faculty of Charles University in Prague, Rector of the University Church of St Saviour and President of the Czech Christian Academy. In 1998 was appointed member of the European Academy of Science and the Arts. In 2002 he was awarded the Andrew Elias Human Tolerance Award "for outstanding services in disseminating the values of tolerance and spiritual and intellectual freedom", 2002 Cardinal König Award, 2010 the Romano Guardini Prize and the 2014 Templeton prize.

Pavel Hošek Th.D. (born 1973) graduated from Charles University in Prague in theology and religious studies. Since 2003 he teaches religious studies at the Protestant Theological Faculty of Charles University in Prague. He is an ordained minister of the Brethren Church and Vicepresident of the Czech Christian Academy. In his publications and scholarly work he focuses on theological interpretation of contemporary culture, on the possible avenues of dialogue between faith and culture and on interfaith relations.

Pavel Roubík (born 1985) is ThD candidate in systematic theology at Charles University in Prague. He studied Protestant theology in Prague and Marburg (2011-2012) and graduated from Charles University in Prague (2013). He engages in theology of history, hermeneutical theology and philosophy of religion, religion and (inter)subjectivity, religion as an interpretation of life and the core of culture vs. theology of revelation, psychology and sociology of religion and religion in the context of art and aesthetics.

Martin Kočí (born 1987) is a PhD candidate in systematic theology at Catholic University Leuven, Belgium. He writes his dissertation on the topic of theological questioning from a post-totalitarian perspective. Martin's main research interests are philosophical theology, theological epistemology and theology in a postmodern context. He is also involved as a lecturer in the Centre of Theology, Philosophy and Media Theory at the Catholic Theological Faculty, Charles University in Prague.

INDEX

A

Aquinas, 102
Arendt, 55, 60, 108, 123
atheism, 3-4, 9, 16, 26, 30, 40, 42, 57, 60, 68, 87, 97, 99, 103, 112-117, 120-123-127, 129
authenticity, 81

B

baptism, 91
Barth, 63-78
believers, 2-3, 9, 24-27, 34, 44, 66, 78, 82-83, 88, 105-109, 114, 121, 125, 133
Bělohradský, 72-78
Benedict XVI, 4, 13, 36, 39, 42, 54, 97, 106, 110, 119, 128
Berger, 17-18, 31, 41, 55, 60, 71, 102, 123
Bible, 7, 33, 54, 101
Boeve, 83-88, 92-93, 104, 112, 114, 123
Bolshevism, 38
Bolzano, 107
Bosch, 32, 33, 36, 39
Brezhnev, 43

C

Čapek, 3, 107
Caputo, 9, 86, 92-93
Catholicism, 4, 15, 52-53, 57, 96, 98-100, 111, 127
Christendom, 34, 53, 130
Christianity, 3-10, 33-36, 44, 46, 53-61, 64, 67-68, 70, 74-77, 83-84, 87, 89-90, 93, 96-98, 100-104, 114, 116-117, 119, 120, 122-123, 127-128, 130

communication, 1, 7, 9, 35, 51-52, 60-61, 75-76, 85
communism, 5, 7, 19-25, 28-29, 32-34, 37-38, 40, 43-44, 47-48, 50-51, 57, 60-61, 105, 108-109
community, 4, 29, 35-36, 99, 112, 119
cultural revolution, 59, 128
Czechoslovakia, 8, 18-22, 37, 43-44, 50, 108

D

D'Costa, 87, 93
Dalferth, 70, 78
Davie, 17, 18, 31
democracy, 50-52, 58, 75
Derrida, 9, 86
desacralisation, 54, 101
Desmond, 106, 123
dialogue, 1, 5, 8-9, 31-38, 41, 52, 54, 82, 91, 107, 110, 112, 120, 122, 127-129, 133
Dierken, 61-62, 66, 69, 72, 78-79
dilemma, 57, 130
dwellers, 2-4, 9, 58, 84, 90-91, 113, 120, 125-127

E

ecumenism, 44
Engels, 43, 47
Enlightenment, 8, 32, 33, 38, 54, 56, 59-60, 64, 67-69, 96, 101-102, 128
ethics, 59, 73, 126, 129
Europe, 5, 8, 14, 17-18, 31-32, 37, 41-44, 47, 49, 51-54, 57-58, 60-61, 72, 77, 84-85, 89,

93, 96-97, 101, 103, 108, 120, 126, 130
Evangelization, 82, 119

F

faith, 2-6, 9, 15, 19, 22, 26-28, 30, 34-37, 39, 48, 52-58, 60, 64, 68, 73, 82-91, 95-98, 100-107, 110-122, 125-130, 133
family, 6, 29, 35, 38, 58, 77
Fasora, 16, 41
Fiala, 10, 14-16, 19, 22-25, 28, 40-41
Fokas, 17-18, 31, 41
Francis, 13, 34, 36, 42, 52, 130
friendship, 35-36
Frühwald, 62, 79
fundamentalism, 8, 57, 97, 115, 128

G

Gauchet, 55, 60
globalisation, 51-52, 60
Gogarten, 67, 79, 100, 123
Gospel, 5-6, 10, 49, 64, 116, 119, 130
Graf, 71, 79

H

Habermas, 62, 79, 128, 131
Hahn, 69, 79
Halík, 1, 3-4, 6-11, 38, 41, 81, 89-93, 96-124, 130-133
Hamplová, 2, 11, 14-17, 20, 26, 30, 40-41
Hanuš, 16-17, 23-25, 41-42
Havel, 3, 45, 47-48, 52, 72, 75, 107
Havlíček, 3, 107
Heisenberg, 118, 124
Hejdánek, 63, 79
hermeneutics, 4-9, 13, 31, 41, 122, 127

Hervieu-Léger, 37, 41
Hošek, 1, 7, 13, 63, 79, 133
Hromádka, 63, 79
humanism, 4, 8, 34, 44, 52, 56, 99, 101-102, 108, 127, 128

I

individualism, 34, 100, 115

J

Jandourek, 105, 124
Joas, 64, 71, 79
John Paul II, 13, 42, 46, 48, 52, 119
John XXIII., 13, 42
Judaism, 53, 99, 116

K

Kaufmann, 55, 60
Kearney, 9, 86-89, 93, 122
kenosis, 100, 131
kenotic, 4-6, 10, 130
knowledge, 32, 39, 92, 117, 119, 121
Kočí, 8-9, 81-82, 85, 89, 95, 133
Körtner, 70, 79
Kovář, 99, 124

L

Lamberigts, 86, 93
language, 4, 6-9, 55-58, 60, 72, 78, 82-91, 97, 103, 105, 115, 118, 129
Lash, 83, 93, 117, 122, 124
Laube, 68, 79
Lauster, 61, 67-68, 79
Lehmann, 62, 67, 71, 79, 80
liberalism, 50, 57, 97, 99
literature, 27, 30, 89-90
Lübbe, 62, 80
Luckmann, 66, 80, 102, 123-124
Luke, 111

Lužný, 14, 41
Lyotard, 83, 88, 93

M

Macek, 78, 80
Malý, 45, 109
Marcel, 55, 60, 105, 118, 124
Marion, 9, 86, 94
Marxism, 43-44, 47, 50, 103, 128
Masaryk, 3, 19, 107
McLean, 81, 84, 94
mentality, 44, 46, 50, 98, 120
metaphor, 4, 13, 28, 29, 31, 41, 89, 110, 129
Metz, 112, 124
Middle Ages, 53-54
Milbank, 104, 124
modernity, 4, 33, 38, 53, 61, 63-65, 68-72, 77, 85, 92, 96, 98, 103, 117-118, 127-128
Myers, 85, 91, 94
mystery, 85, 88, 91, 114-115, 118-119, 121, 129

N

nationalism, 56, 58
Nazism, 38, 46, 56
Nešporová, 13-23, 26, 30, 40-42

O

Olivetti, 88, 92, 94
otherness, 87, 118, 122
Otto, 91

P

Palacký, 107
Pannenberg, 65, 67, 80
Patočka, 107, 117-118, 124
Paul VI, 13, 42
persecution, 15, 20, 22, 44, 48-49, 57, 60, 97
pietism, 58

Pippin, 117, 124
Pius IX, 98
postmodern, 9, 10, 33, 81-89, 91-92, 96, 98, 100, 102, 112, 117-122, 128, 133
Protestant, 14, 16, 24, 26, 45, 50, 56, 63, 75, 78, 133
Prudký, 29, 35, 42, 109, 124

Q

Quesnell, 17, 32, 40, 42

R

rationalism, 32-33, 56, 91, 98, 118
Ratzinger, 119, 128, 129, 131
religion, 1-3, 8, 13-18, 20, 22, 25-31, 35, 43-44, 52-53, 55-60, 62-64, 66, 68-72, 74-77, 82, 85-89, 95-108, 115, 120, 122, 125, 127-130, 133
religiosity, 9, 13-30, 40, 42, 59, 63, 69, 71, 85, 96, 107-108, 115, 125
Rendtorff, 67-68, 75, 80
revelation, 5, 68, 121, 133
ritual, 30, 76
Roubík, 1, 8, 9, 61, 89, 95, 133

S

Schleiermacher, 63, 66, 69, 80, 102, 124
science, 29, 32, 52, 56-57, 59, 65, 73, 90, 97, 118, 128-129
secular, 2, 4-5, 8-9, 13, 31, 33-34, 49, 52-60, 62, 67-68, 78, 82-83, 89, 96-98, 101, 108, 113, 122, 127-128
secularization, 8, 54-56, 59, 62-69, 77, 83, 95-96, 99-100, 102-103, 110, 120, 122
Sedláčková, 23, 42

seekers, 2-5, 8-10, 31, 33-34, 36-38, 40-41, 52, 58, 81-84, 87-92, 110-112, 119-120, 125-129
Simmel, 70, 78, 80
Smolík, 64, 80
socialism, 21-22, 43, 51, 99
Sokol, 62, 72-74, 77-78, 80
Soviet Union, 21, 43
spirituality, 2, 13, 28, 30-31, 40-41, 58, 60, 98, 111, 115, 122, 125
Spousta, 17, 23-25, 42
Sprondel, 61, 80
Štampach, 24, 42
Sullivan, 84, 93-94
Sundermeier, 104, 124
superstructure, 43, 50, 55
symbols, 16, 31, 56, 58, 76, 89

T

Taylor, 1-2, 11, 56, 60, 81-84, 94-95, 102, 124
technology, 8, 32, 57, 69, 73, 116
theology, 7, 49, 57-58, 63-64, 70, 82, 85-87, 90, 97-98, 100, 104, 110-112, 114-122, 127, 129, 133
Tichý, 11-14, 38, 42
tolerance, 44, 101, 129, 133
Tomášek, 45-47, 109
totalitarianism, 45, 47, 108-109, 118

transcendent, 5, 54, 60, 69, 74, 107-108, 128
Trinity, 25, 36
triumphalist, 4-5, 110, 119, 129
truth, 16, 18, 34, 43, 47-48, 57, 90, 92, 97, 104, 113-115

V

Václavík, 14-21, 29, 30, 42
values, 5-6, 13, 30-33, 35-36, 39, 44, 46, 49, 59, 60, 62, 71, 77, 103, 107, 111, 133
Vaško, 20, 37
Vatican Council II, 41, 57, 97-98, 115, 126-128
Vávra, 11, 14, 38, 42
Velvet Revolution, 22-23, 45

W

Wallace, 95, 124
Warsaw Pact, 21, 43
Weber, 50, 62, 64-65
Williams, 9, 85, 88, 90, 94
wisdom, 37, 91, 92, 101, 119, 122
Wojtyla, 46

Z

Zacchaeus, 9, 81, 93, 110-111, 120
Zakaria, 55, 60
Zinovjev, 48, 52

THE COUNCIL FOR RESEARCH IN VALUES AND PHILOSOPHY

PURPOSE

Today there is urgent need to attend to the nature and dignity of the person, to the quality of human life, to the purpose and goal of the physical transformation of our environment, and to the relation of all this to the development of social and political life. This, in turn, requires philosophic clarification of the base upon which freedom is exercised, that is, of the values which provide stability and guidance to one's decisions.

Such studies must be able to reach deeply into one's culture and that of other parts of the world as mutually reinforcing and enriching in order to uncover the roots of the dignity of persons and of their societies. They must be able to identify the conceptual forms in terms of which modern industrial and technological developments are structured and how these impact upon human self-understanding. Above all, they must be able to bring these elements together in the creative understanding essential for setting our goals and determining our modes of interaction. In the present complex global circumstances this is a condition for growing together with trust and justice, honest dedication and mutual concern.

The Council for Studies in Values and Philosophy (RVP) unites scholars who share these concerns and are interested in the application thereto of existing capabilities in the field of philosophy and other disciplines. Its work is to identify areas in which study is needed, the intellectual resources which can be brought to bear thereupon, and the means for publication and interchange of the work from the various regions of the world. In bringing these together its goal is scientific discovery and publication which contributes to the present promotion of humankind.

In sum, our times present both the need and the opportunity for deeper and ever more progressive understanding of the person and of the foundations of social life. The development of such understanding is the goal of the RVP.

PROJECTS

A set of related research efforts is currently in process:

1. *Cultural Heritage and Contemporary Change: Philosophical Foundations for Social Life.* Focused, mutually coordinated research teams in university centers prepare volumes as part of an integrated philosophic search for self-understanding differentiated by culture and civilization. These evolve more adequate understandings of the person in society and look to the cultural heritage of each for the resources to respond to the challenges of its own specific contemporary transformation.

2. *Seminars on Culture and Contemporary Issues*. This series of 10 week crosscultural and interdisciplinary seminars is coordinated by the RVP in Washington.

3. *Joint-Colloquia* with Institutes of Philosophy of the National Academies of Science, university philosophy departments, and societies. Underway since 1976 in Eastern Europe and, since 1987, in China, these concern the person in contemporary society.

4. *Foundations of Moral Education and Character Development.* A study in values and education which unites philosophers, psychologists, social scientists and scholars in education in the elaboration of ways of enriching the moral content of education and character development. This work has been underway since 1980.

The personnel for these projects consists of established scholars willing to contribute their time and research as part of their professional commitment to life in contemporary society. For resources to implement this work the Council, as 501 C3 a non-profit organization incorporated in the District of Colombia, looks to various private foundations, public programs and enterprises.

PUBLICATIONS ON CULTURAL HERITAGE AND CONTEMPORARY CHANGE

Series I. Culture and Values
Series II. African Philosophical Studies
Series IIA. Islamic Philosophical Studies
Series III. Asian Philosophical Studies
Series IV. Western European Philosophical Studies
Series IVA. Central and Eastern European Philosophical Studies
Series V. Latin American Philosophical Studies
Series VI. Foundations of Moral Education
Series VII. Seminars: Culture and Values
Series VIII. Christian Philosophical Studies

****

CULTURAL HERITAGE AND CONTEMPORARY CHANGE

Series I. Culture and Values

I.1 *Research on Culture and Values: Intersection of Universities, Churches and Nations.* George F. McLean, ed. ISBN 0819173533 (paper); 081917352-5 (cloth).

I.2 *The Knowledge of Values: A Methodological Introduction to the Study of Values;* A. Lopez Quintas, ed. ISBN 081917419x (paper); 0819174181 (cloth).

I.3 *Reading Philosophy for the XXIst Century.* George F. McLean, ed. ISBN 0819174157 (paper); 0819174149 (cloth).
I.4 *Relations between Cultures.* John A. Kromkowski, ed. ISBN 1565180089 (paper); 1565180097 (cloth).
I.5 *Urbanization and Values.* John A. Kromkowski, ed. ISBN 1565180100 (paper); 1565180119 (cloth).
I.6 *The Place of the Person in Social Life.* Paul Peachey and John A. Kromkowski, eds. ISBN 1565180127 (paper); 156518013-5 (cloth).
I.7 *Abrahamic Faiths, Ethnicity and Ethnic Conflicts.* Paul Peachey, George F. McLean and John A. Kromkowski, eds. ISBN 1565181042 (paper).
I.8 *Ancient Western Philosophy: The Hellenic Emergence.* George F. McLean and Patrick J. Aspell, eds. ISBN 156518100X (paper).
I.9 *Medieval Western Philosophy: The European Emergence.* Patrick J. Aspell, ed. ISBN 1565180941 (paper).
I.10 *The Ethical Implications of Unity and the Divine in Nicholas of Cusa.* David L. De Leonardis. ISBN 1565181123 (paper).
I.11 *Ethics at the Crossroads: 1.Normative Ethics and Objective Reason.* George F. McLean, ed. ISBN 1565180224 (paper).
I.12 *Ethics at the Crossroads: 2. Personalist Ethics and Human Subjectivity.* George F. McLean, ed. ISBN 1565180240 (paper).
I.13 *The Emancipative Theory of Jürgen Habermas and Metaphysics.* Robert Badillo. ISBN 1565180429 (paper); 1565180437 (cloth).
I.14 *The Deficient Cause of Moral Evil According to Thomas Aquinas.* Edward Cook. ISBN 1565180704 (paper).
I.15 *Human Love: Its Meaning and Scope, a Phenomenology of Gift and Encounter.* Alfonso Lopez Quintas. ISBN 1565180747 (paper).
I.16 *Civil Society and Social Reconstruction.* George F. McLean, ed. ISBN 1565180860 (paper).
I.17 *Ways to God, Personal and Social at the Turn of Millennia: The Iqbal Lecture, Lahore.* George F. McLean. ISBN 1565181239 (paper).
I.18 *The Role of the Sublime in Kant's Moral Metaphysics.* John R. Goodreau. ISBN 1565181247 (paper).
I.19 *Philosophical Challenges and Opportunities of Globalization.* Oliva Blanchette, Tomonobu Imamichi and George F. McLean, eds. ISBN 1565181298 (paper).
I.20 *Faith, Reason and Philosophy: Lectures at The al-Azhar, Qom, Tehran, Lahore and Beijing; Appendix: The Encyclical Letter: Fides et Ratio.* George F. McLean. ISBN 156518130 (paper).
I.21 *Religion and the Relation between Civilizations: Lectures on Cooperation between Islamic and Christian Cultures in a Global Horizon.* George F. McLean. ISBN 1565181522 (paper).
I.22 *Freedom, Cultural Traditions and Progress: Philosophy in Civil Society and Nation Building, Tashkent Lectures, 1999.* George F. McLean. ISBN 1565181514 (paper).
I.23 *Ecology of Knowledge.* Jerzy A. Wojciechowski. ISBN 1565181581 (paper).

I.24 *God and the Challenge of Evil: A Critical Examination of Some Serious Objections to the Good and Omnipotent God*. John L. Yardan. ISBN 1565181603 (paper).
I.25 *Reason, Rationality and Reasonableness, Vietnamese Philosophical Studies, I*. Tran Van Doan. ISBN 1565181662 (paper).
I.26 *The Culture of Citizenship: Inventing Postmodern Civic Culture*. Thomas Bridges. ISBN 1565181689 (paper).
I.27 *The Historicity of Understanding and the Problem of Relativism in Gadamer's Philosophical Hermeneutics*. Osman Bilen. ISBN 1565181670 (paper).
I.28 *Speaking of God*. Carlo Huber. ISBN 1565181697 (paper).
I.29 *Persons, Peoples and Cultures in a Global Age: Metaphysical Bases for Peace between Civilizations*. George F. McLean. ISBN 1565181875 (paper).
I.30 *Hermeneutics, Tradition and Contemporary Change: Lectures in Chennai/Madras, India*. George F. McLean. ISBN 1565181883 (paper).
I.31 *Husserl and Stein*. Richard Feist and William Sweet, eds. ISBN 1565181948 (paper).
I.32 *Paul Hanly Furfey's Quest for a Good Society*. Bronislaw Misztal, Francesco Villa, and Eric Sean Williams, eds. ISBN 1565182278 (paper).
I.33 *Three Theories of Society*. Paul Hanly Furfey. ISBN 9781565182288 (paper).
I.34 *Building Peace in Civil Society: An Autobiographical Report from a Believers' Church*. Paul Peachey. ISBN 9781565182325 (paper).
I.35 *Karol Wojtyla's Philosophical Legacy*. Agnes B. Curry, Nancy Mardas and George F. McLean, eds. ISBN 9781565182479 (paper).
I.36 *Kantian Form and Phenomenological Force: Kant's Imperatives and the Directives of Contemporary Phenomenology*. Randolph C. Wheeler. ISBN 9781565182547 (paper).
I.37 *Beyond Modernity: The Recovery of Person and Community in Global Times: Lectures in China and Vietnam*. George F. McLean. ISBN 9781565182578 (paper)
I. 38 *Religion and Culture*. George F. McLean. ISBN 9781565182561 (paper).
I.39 *The Dialogue of Cultural Traditions: Global Perspective*. William Sweet, George F. McLean, Tomonobu Imamichi, Safak Ural, O. Faruk Akyol, eds. ISBN 9781565182585 (paper).
I.40 *Unity and Harmony, Love and Compassion in Global Times*. George F. McLean. ISBN 9781565182592 (paper).
I.41 *Intercultural Dialogue and Human Rights*. Luigi Bonanate, Roberto Papini and William Sweet, eds. ISBN 9781565182714 (paper).
I.42 *Philosophy Emerging from Culture*. William Sweet, George F. McLean, Oliva Blanchette, Wonbin Park, eds. ISBN 9781565182851 (paper).

I.43 *Whence Intelligibility?* Louis Perron, ed. ISBN 9781565182905 (paper).
I.44 *What is Intercultural Philosophy?* William Sweet, ed. ISBN 9781565182912 (paper).

Series II. African Philosophical Studies

II.1 *Person and Community: Ghanaian Philosophical Studies: I.* Kwasi Wiredu and Kwame Gyekye, eds. ISBN 1565180046 (paper); 1565180054 (cloth).
II.2 *The Foundations of Social Life: Ugandan Philosophical Studies: I.* A.T. Dalfovo, ed. ISBN 1565180062 (paper); 156518007-0 (cloth).
II.3 *Identity and Change in Nigeria: Nigerian Philosophical Studies, I.* Theophilus Okere, ed. ISBN 1565180682 (paper).
II.4 *Social Reconstruction in Africa: Ugandan Philosophical studies, II.* E. Wamala, A.R. Byaruhanga, A.T. Dalfovo, J.K. Kigongo, S.A. Mwanahewa and G. Tusabe, eds. ISBN 1565181182 (paper).
II.5 *Ghana: Changing Values/Changing Technologies: Ghanaian Philosophical Studies, II.* Helen Lauer, ed. ISBN 1565181441 (paper).
II.6 *Sameness and Difference: Problems and Potentials in South African Civil Society: South African Philosophical Studies, I.* James R. Cochrane and Bastienne Klein, eds. ISBN 1565181557 (paper).
II.7 *Protest and Engagement: Philosophy after Apartheid at an Historically Black South African University: South African Philosophical Studies, II.* Patrick Giddy, ed. ISBN 1565181638 (paper).
II.8 *Ethics, Human Rights and Development in Africa: Ugandan Philosophical Studies, III.* A.T. Dalfovo, J.K. Kigongo, J. Kisekka, G. Tusabe, E. Wamala, R. Munyonyo, A.B. Rukooko, A.B.T. Byaruhanga-akiiki, and M. Mawa, eds. ISBN 1565181727 (paper).
II.9 *Beyond Cultures: Perceiving a Common Humanity: Ghanaian Philosophical Studies, III.* Kwame Gyekye. ISBN 156518193X (paper).
II.10 *Social and Religious Concerns of East African: A Wajibu Anthology: Kenyan Philosophical Studies, I.* Gerald J. Wanjohi and G. Wakuraya Wanjohi, eds. ISBN 1565182219 (paper).
II.11 *The Idea of an African University: The Nigerian Experience: Nigerian Philosophical Studies, II.* Joseph Kenny, ed. ISBN 9781565182301 (paper).
II.12 *The Struggles after the Struggle: Zimbabwean Philosophical Study, I.* David Kaulemu, ed. ISBN 9781565182318 (paper).
II.13 *Indigenous and Modern Environmental Ethics: A Study of the Indigenous Oromo Environmental Ethic and Modern Issues of Environment and Development: Ethiopian Philosophical Studies, I.* Workineh Kelbessa. ISBN 9781565182530 (paper).

II.14 *African Philosophy and the Future of Africa: South African Philosophical Studies, III.* Gerard Walmsley, ed. ISMB 9781565182707 (paper).
II.15 *Philosophy in Ethiopia: African Philosophy Today, I: Ethiopian Philosophical Studies, II.* Bekele Gutema and Charles C. Verharen, eds. ISBN 9781565182790 (paper).
II.16 *The Idea of a Nigerian University: A Revisited: Nigerian Philosophical Studies, III.* Olatunji Oyeshile and Joseph Kenny, eds. ISBN 9781565182776 (paper).
II.17 *Philosophy in African Traditions and Cultures, Zimbabwe Philosophical Studies, II.* Fainos Mangena, Tarisayi Andrea Chimuka, Francis Mabiri, eds. ISBN 9781565182998 (paper).

Series IIA. Islamic Philosophical Studies

IIA.1 *Islam and the Political Order.* Muhammad Saïd al-Ashmawy. ISBN ISBN 156518047X (paper); 156518046-1 (cloth).
IIA.2 *Al-Ghazali Deliverance from Error and Mystical Union with the Almighty: Al-munqidh Min al-Dadāl.* Critical Arabic edition and English translation by Muhammad Abulaylah and Nurshif Abdul-Rahim Rifat; Introduction and notes by George F. McLean. ISBN 1565181530 (Arabic-English edition, paper), ISBN 1565180828 (Arabic edition, paper), ISBN 156518081X (English edition, paper)
IIA.3 *Philosophy in Pakistan.* Naeem Ahmad, ed. ISBN 1565181085 (paper).
IIA.4 *The Authenticity of the Text in Hermeneutics.* Seyed Musa Dibadj. ISBN 1565181174 (paper).
IIA.5 *Interpretation and the Problem of the Intention of the Author: H.-G. Gadamer vs E.D. Hirsch.* Burhanettin Tatar. ISBN 156518121 (paper).
IIA.6 *Ways to God, Personal and Social at the Turn of Millennia: The Iqbal Lectures, Lahore.* George F. McLean. ISBN 1565181239 (paper).
IIA.7 *Faith, Reason and Philosophy: Lectures at Al-Azhar University, Qom, Tehran, Lahore and Beijing; Appendix: The Encyclical Letter: Fides et Ratio.* George F. McLean. ISBN 1565181301 (paper).
IIA.8 *Islamic and Christian Cultures: Conflict or Dialogue: Bulgarian Philosophical Studies, III.* Plament Makariev, ed. ISBN 156518162X (paper).
IIA.9 *Values of Islamic Culture and the Experience of History, Russian Philosophical Studies, I.* Nur Kirabaev, Yuriy Pochta, eds. ISBN 1565181336 (paper).
IIA.10 *Christian-Islamic Preambles of Faith.* Joseph Kenny. ISBN 1565181387 (paper).
IIA.11 *The Historicity of Understanding and the Problem of Relativism in Gadamer's Philosophical Hermeneutics.* Osman Bilen. ISBN 1565181670 (paper).

IIA.12 *Religion and the Relation between Civilizations: Lectures on Cooperation between Islamic and Christian Cultures in a Global Horizon.* George F. McLean. ISBN 1565181522 (paper).
IIA.13 *Modern Western Christian Theological Understandings of Muslims since the Second Vatican Council.* Mahmut Aydin. ISBN 1565181719 (paper).
IIA.14 *Philosophy of the Muslim World; Authors and Principal Themes.* Joseph Kenny. ISBN 1565181794 (paper).
IIA.15 *Islam and Its Quest for Peace: Jihad, Justice and Education.* Mustafa Köylü. ISBN 1565181808 (paper).
IIA.16 *Islamic Thought on the Existence of God: Contributions and Contrasts with Contemporary Western Philosophy of Religion.* Cafer S. Yaran. ISBN 1565181921 (paper).
IIA.17 *Hermeneutics, Faith, and Relations between Cultures: Lectures in Qom, Iran.* George F. McLean. ISBN 1565181913 (paper).
IIA.18 *Change and Essence: Dialectical Relations between Change and Continuity in the Turkish Intellectual Tradition.* Sinasi Gunduz and Cafer S. Yaran, eds. ISBN 1565182227 (paper).
IIA. 19 *Understanding Other Religions: Al-Biruni and Gadamer's "Fusion of Horizons".* Kemal Ataman. ISBN 9781565182523 (paper).

Series III. Asian Philosophical Studies

III.1 *Man and Nature: Chinese Philosophical Studies, I.* Tang Yi-jie and Li Zhen, eds. ISBN 0819174130 (paper); 0819174122 (cloth).
III.2 *Chinese Foundations for Moral Education and Character Development: Chinese Philosophical Studies, II.* Tran van Doan, ed. ISBN 1565180321 (paper); 156518033X (cloth).
III.3 *Confucianism, Buddhism, Taoism, Christianity and Chinese Culture: Chinese Philosophical Studies, III.* Tang Yijie. ISBN 1565180348 (paper); 156518035-6 (cloth).
III.4 *Morality, Metaphysics and Chinese Culture (Metaphysics, Culture and Morality, I).* Vincent Shen and Tran van Doan, eds. ISBN 1565180275 (paper); 156518026-7 (cloth).
III.5 *Tradition, Harmony and Transcendence.* George F. McLean. ISBN 1565180313 (paper); 156518030-5 (cloth).
III.6 *Psychology, Phenomenology and Chinese Philosophy: Chinese Philosophical Studies, VI.* Vincent Shen, Richard Knowles and Tran Van Doan, eds. ISBN 1565180453 (paper); 1565180445 (cloth).
III.7 *Values in Philippine Culture and Education: Philippine Philosophical Studies, I.* Manuel B. Dy, Jr., ed. ISBN 1565180412 (paper); 156518040-2 (cloth).
III.7A *The Human Person and Society: Chinese Philosophical Studies, VIIA.* Zhu Dasheng, Jin Xiping and George F. McLean, eds. ISBN 1565180887.

III.8 *The Filipino Mind: Philippine Philosophical Studies II*. Leonardo N. Mercado. ISBN 156518064X (paper); 156518063-1 (cloth).

III.9 *Philosophy of Science and Education: Chinese Philosophical Studies IX*. Vincent Shen and Tran Van Doan, eds. ISBN 1565180763 (paper); 156518075-5 (cloth).

III.10 *Chinese Cultural Traditions and Modernization: Chinese Philosophical Studies, X*. Wang Miaoyang, Yu Xuanmeng and George F. McLean, eds. ISBN 1565180682 (paper).

III.11 *The Humanization of Technology and Chinese Culture: Chinese Philosophical Studies XI*. Tomonobu Imamichi, Wang Miaoyang and Liu Fangtong, eds. ISBN 1565181166 (paper).

III.12 *Beyond Modernization: Chinese Roots of Global Awareness: Chinese Philosophical Studies, XII*. Wang Miaoyang, Yu Xuanmeng and George F. McLean, eds. ISBN 1565180909 (paper).

III.13 *Philosophy and Modernization in China: Chinese Philosophical Studies XIII*. Liu Fangtong, Huang Songjie and George F. McLean, eds. ISBN 1565180666 (paper).

III.14 *Economic Ethics and Chinese Culture: Chinese Philosophical Studies, XIV*. Yu Xuanmeng, Lu Xiaohe, Liu Fangtong, Zhang Rulun and Georges Enderle, eds. ISBN 1565180925 (paper).

III.15 *Civil Society in a Chinese Context: Chinese Philosophical Studies XV*. Wang Miaoyang, Yu Xuanmeng and Manuel B. Dy, eds. ISBN 1565180844 (paper).

III.16 *The Bases of Values in a Time of Change: Chinese and Western: Chinese Philosophical Studies, XVI*. Kirti Bunchua, Liu Fangtong, Yu Xuanmeng, Yu Wujin, eds. ISBN l56518114X (paper).

III.17 *Dialogue between Christian Philosophy and Chinese Culture: Philosophical Perspectives for the Third Millennium: Chinese Philosophical Studies, XVII*. Paschal Ting, Marian Kao and Bernard Li, eds. ISBN 1565181735 (paper).

III.18 *The Poverty of Ideological Education: Chinese Philosophical Studies, XVIII*. Tran Van Doan. ISBN 1565181646 (paper).

III.19 *God and the Discovery of Man: Classical and Contemporary Approaches: Lectures in Wuhan, China*. George F. McLean. ISBN 1565181891 (paper).

III.20 *Cultural Impact on International Relations: Chinese Philosophical Studies, XX*. Yu Xintian, ed. ISBN 156518176X (paper).

III.21 *Cultural Factors in International Relations: Chinese Philosophical Studies, XXI*. Yu Xintian, ed. ISBN 1565182049 (paper).

III.22 *Wisdom in China and the West: Chinese Philosophical Studies, XXII*. Vincent Shen and Willard Oxtoby. ISBN 1565182057 (paper)

III.23 *China's Contemporary Philosophical Journey: Western Philosophy and Marxism: Chinese Philosophical Studies, XXIII*. Liu Fangtong. ISBN 1565182065 (paper).

III.24 *Shanghai: Its Urbanization and Culture: Chinese Philosophical Studies, XXIV*. Yu Xuanmeng and He Xirong, eds. ISBN 1565182073 (paper).
III.25 *Dialogue of Philosophies, Religions and Civilizations in the Era of Globalization: Chinese Philosophical Studies, XXV*. Zhao Dunhua, ed. ISBN 9781565182431 (paper).
III.26 *Rethinking Marx: Chinese Philosophical Studies, XXVI*. Zou Shipeng and Yang Xuegong, eds. ISBN 9781565182448 (paper).
III.27 *Confucian Ethics in Retrospect and Prospect: Chinese Philosophical Studies XXVII*. Vincent Shen and Kwong-loi Shun, eds. ISBN 9781565182455 (paper).
III.28 *Cultural Tradition and Social Progress, Chinese Philosophical Studies, XXVIII*. He Xirong, Yu Xuanmeng, Yu Xintian, Yu Wujing, Yang Junyi, eds. ISBN 9781565182660 (paper).
III.29 *Spiritual Foundations and Chinese Culture: A Philosophical Approach: Chinese Philosophical Studies, XXIX*. Anthony J. Carroll and Katia Lenehan, eds. ISBN 9781565182974 (paper)
III.30 *Diversity in Unity: Harmony in a Global Age: Chinese Philosophical Studies, XXX*. He Xirong and Yu Xuanmeng, eds. ISBN 9781565183070 (paper).
IIIB.1 *Authentic Human Destiny: The Paths of Shankara and Heidegger: Indian Philosophical Studies, I*. Vensus A. George. ISBN 1565181190 (paper).
IIIB.2 *The Experience of Being as Goal of Human Existence: The Heideggerian Approach: Indian Philosophical Studies, II*. Vensus A. George. ISBN 156518145X (paper).
IIIB.3 *Religious Dialogue as Hermeneutics: Bede Griffiths's Advaitic Approach: Indian Philosophical Studies, III*. Kuruvilla Pandikattu. ISBN 1565181395 (paper).
IIIB.4 *Self-Realization [Brahmaanubhava]: The Advaitic Perspective of Shankara: Indian Philosophical Studies, IV*. Vensus A. George. ISBN 1565181549 (paper).
IIIB.5 *Gandhi: The Meaning of Mahatma for the Millennium: Indian Philosophical Studies, V*. Kuruvilla Pandikattu, ed. ISBN 1565181565 (paper).
IIIB.6 *Civil Society in Indian Cultures: Indian Philosophical Studies, VI*. Asha Mukherjee, Sabujkali Sen (Mitra) and K. Bagchi, eds. ISBN 1565181573 (paper).
IIIB.7 *Hermeneutics, Tradition and Contemporary Change: Lectures in Chennai/Madras, India*. George F. McLean. ISBN 1565181883 (paper).
IIIB.8 *Plenitude and Participation: The Life of God in Man: Lectures in Chennai/Madras, India*. George F. McLean. ISBN 1565181999 (paper).
IIIB.9 *Sufism and Bhakti, a Comparative Study: Indian Philosophical Studies, VII*. Md. Sirajul Islam. ISBN 1565181980 (paper).

IIIB.10 *Reasons for Hope: Its Nature, Role and Future*: Indian Philosophical Studies, *VIII*. Kuruvilla Pandikattu, ed. ISBN 156518 2162 (paper).
IIIB.11 *Lifeworlds and Ethics: Studies in Several Keys*: Indian Philosophical Studies, *IX*. Margaret Chatterjee. ISBN 9781565182332 (paper).
IIIB.12 *Paths to the Divine: Ancient and Indian*: Indian Philosophical Studies, *X*. Vensus A. George. ISBN 9781565182486 (paper).
IIB.13 *Faith, Reason, Science: Philosophical Reflections with Special Reference to Fides et Ratio*: Indian Philosophical Studies, *XIII*. Varghese Manimala, ed. IBSN 9781565182554 (paper).
IIIB.14 *Identity, Creativity and Modernization: Perspectives on Indian Cultural Tradition: Indian Philosophical Studies, XIV*. Sebastian Velassery and Vensus A. George, eds. ISBN 9781565182783 (paper).
IIIB.15 *Elusive Transcendence: An Exploration of the Human Condition Based on Paul Ricoeur: Indian Philosophical Studies, XV*. Kuruvilla Pandikattu. ISBN 9781565182950 (paper).
IIIC.1 *Spiritual Values and Social Progress: Uzbekistan Philosophical Studies, I*. Said Shermukhamedov and Victoriya Levinskaya, eds. ISBN 1565181433 (paper).
IIIC.2 *Kazakhstan: Cultural Inheritance and Social Transformation: Kazakh Philosophical Studies, I*. Abdumalik Nysanbayev. ISBN 1565182022 (paper).
IIIC.3 *Social Memory and Contemporaneity: Kyrgyz Philosophical Studies, I*. Gulnara A. Bakieva. ISBN 9781565182349 (paper).
IIID.1 *Reason, Rationality and Reasonableness: Vietnamese Philosophical Studies, I*. Tran Van Doan. ISBN 1565181662 (paper).
IIID.2 *Hermeneutics for a Global Age: Lectures in Shanghai and Hanoi*. George F. McLean. ISBN 1565181905 (paper).
IIID.3 *Cultural Traditions and Contemporary Challenges in Southeast Asia*. Warayuth Sriwarakuel, Manuel B. Dy, J. Haryatmoko, Nguyen Trong Chuan, and Chhay Yiheang, eds. ISBN 1565182138 (paper).
IIID.4 *Filipino Cultural Traits: Claro R. Ceniza Lectures*. Rolando M. Gripaldo, ed. ISBN 1565182251 (paper).
IIID.5 *The History of Buddhism in Vietnam*. Chief editor: Nguyen Tai Thu; Authors: Dinh Minh Chi, Ly Kim Hoa, Ha thuc Minh, Ha Van Tan, Nguyen Tai Thu. ISBN 1565180984 (paper).
IIID.6 *Relations between Religions and Cultures in Southeast Asia*. Gadis Arivia and Donny Gahral Adian, eds. ISBN 9781565182509 (paper).

Series IV. Western European Philosophical Studies

IV.1 *Italy in Transition: The Long Road from the First to the Second Republic: The Edmund D. Pellegrino Lectures*. Paolo Janni, ed. ISBN 1565181204 (paper).

IV.2 *Italy and the European Monetary Union: The Edmund D. Pellegrino Lectures*. Paolo Janni, ed. ISBN 156518128X (paper).
IV.3 *Italy at the Millennium: Economy, Politics, Literature and Journalism: The Edmund D. Pellegrino Lectures*. Paolo Janni, ed. ISBN 1565181581 (paper).
IV.4 *Speaking of God*. Carlo Huber. ISBN 1565181697 (paper).
IV.5 *The Essence of Italian Culture and the Challenge of a Global Age*. Paulo Janni and George F. McLean, eds. ISBB 1565181778 (paper).
IV.6 *Italic Identity in Pluralistic Contexts: Toward the Development of Intercultural Competencies*. Piero Bassetti and Paolo Janni, eds. ISBN 1565181441 (paper).
IV.7 *Phenomenon of Affectivity: Phenomenological-Anthropological Perspectives*. Ghislaine Florival. ISBN 9781565182899 (paper).
IV.8 *Towards a Kenotic Vision of Authority in the Catholic Church*. Anthony J. Carroll, Marthe Kerkwijk, Michael Kirwan, James Sweeney, eds ISNB 9781565182936 (paper).
IV.9 *A Catholic Minority Church in a World of Seekers*. Staf Hellemans and Peter Jonkers, eds. ISBN 9781565183018 (paper).

Series IVA. Central and Eastern European Philosophical Studies

IVA.1 *The Philosophy of Person: Solidarity and Cultural Creativity: Polish Philosophical Studies, I*. A. Tischner, J.M. Zycinski, eds. ISBN 1565180496 (paper); 156518048-8 (cloth).
IVA.2 *Public and Private Social Inventions in Modern Societies: Polish Philosophical Studies, II*. L. Dyczewski, P. Peachey, J.A. Kromkowski, eds. ISBN. 1565180518 (paper); 156518050X (cloth).
IVA.3 *Traditions and Present Problems of Czech Political Culture: Czechoslovak Philosophical Studies, I*. M. Bednár and M. Vejraka, eds. ISBN 1565180577 (paper); 156518056-9 (cloth).
IVA.4 *Czech Philosophy in the XXth Century: Czech Philosophical Studies, II*. Lubomír Nový and Jirí Gabriel, eds. ISBN 1565180291 (paper); 156518028-3 (cloth).
IVA.5 *Language, Values and the Slovak Nation: Slovak Philosophical Studies, I*. Tibor Pichler and Jana Gašparí-ková, eds. ISBN 1565180372 (paper); 156518036-4 (cloth).
IVA.6 *Morality and Public Life in a Time of Change: Bulgarian Philosophical Studies, I*. V. Prodanov and A. Davidov, eds. ISBN 1565180550 (paper); 1565180542 (cloth).
IVA.7 *Knowledge and Morality: Georgian Philosophical Studies, 1*. N.V. Chavchavadze, G. Nodia and P. Peachey, eds. ISBN 1565180534 (paper); 1565180526 (cloth).
IVA.8 *Cultural Heritage and Social Change: Lithuanian Philosophical Studies, I*. Bronius Kuzmickas and Aleksandr Dobrynin, eds. ISBN 1565180399 (paper); 1565180380 (cloth).

IVA.9 *National, Cultural and Ethnic Identities: Harmony beyond Conflict: Czech Philosophical Studies, III.* Jaroslav Hroch, David Hollan, George F. McLean, eds. ISBN 1565181131 (paper).
IVA.10 *Models of Identities in Postcommunist Societies: Yugoslav Philosophical Studies, I.* Zagorka Golubovic and George F. McLean, eds. ISBN 1565181211 (paper).
IVA.11 *Interests and Values: The Spirit of Venture in a Time of Change: Slovak Philosophical Studies, II.* Tibor Pichler and Jana Gasparikova, eds. ISBN 1565181255 (paper).
IVA.12 *Creating Democratic Societies: Values and Norms: Bulgarian Philosophical Studies, II.* Plamen Makariev, Andrew M. Blasko and Asen Davidov, eds. ISBN 156518131X (paper).
IVA.13 *Values of Islamic Culture and the Experience of History: Russian Philosophical Studies, I.* Nur Kirabaev and Yuriy Pochta, eds. ISBN 1565181336 (paper).
IVA.14 *Values and Education in Romania Today: Romanian Philosophical Studies, I.* Marin Calin and Magdalena Dumitrana, eds. ISBN 1565181344 (paper).
IVA.15 *Between Words and Reality, Studies on the Politics of Recognition and the Changes of Regime in Contemporary Romania: Romanian Philosophical Studies, II.* Victor Neumann. ISBN 1565181611 (paper).
IVA.16 *Culture and Freedom: Romanian Philosophical Studies, III.* Marin Aiftinca, ed. ISBN 1565181360 (paper).
IVA.17 *Lithuanian Philosophy: Persons and Ideas: Lithuanian Philosophical Studies, II.* Jurate Baranova, ed. ISBN 1565181379 (paper).
IVA.18 *Human Dignity: Values and Justice: Czech Philosophical Studies, IV.* Miloslav Bednar, ed. ISBN 1565181409 (paper).
IVA.19 *Values in the Polish Cultural Tradition: Polish Philosophical Studies, III.* Leon Dyczewski, ed. ISBN 1565181425 (paper).
IVA.20 *Liberalization and Transformation of Morality in Post-communist Countries: Polish Philosophical Studies, IV.* Tadeusz Buksinski. ISBN 1565181786 (paper).
IVA.21 *Islamic and Christian Cultures: Conflict or Dialogue: Bulgarian Philosophical Studies, III.* Plament Makariev, ed. ISBN 156518162X (paper).
IVA.22 *Moral, Legal and Political Values in Romanian Culture: Romanian Philosophical Studies, IV.* Mihaela Czobor-Lupp and J. Stefan Lupp, eds. ISBN 1565181700 (paper).
IVA.23 *Social Philosophy: Paradigm of Contemporary Thinking: Lithuanian Philosophical Studies, III.* Jurate Morkuniene. ISBN 1565182030 (paper).
IVA.24 *Romania: Cultural Identity and Education for Civil Society: Romanian Philosophical Studies, V.* Magdalena Dumitrana, ed. ISBN 156518209X (paper).

IVA.25 *Polish Axiology: the 20th Century and Beyond: Polish Philosophical Studies, V.* Stanislaw Jedynak, ed. ISBN 1565181417 (paper).
IVA.26 *Contemporary Philosophical Discourse in Lithuania: Lithuanian Philosophical Studies, IV.* Jurate Baranova, ed. ISBN 156518-2154 (paper).
IVA.27 *Eastern Europe and the Challenges of Globalization: Polish Philosophical Studies, VI.* Tadeusz Buksinski and Dariusz Dobrzanski, ed. ISBN 1565182189 (paper).
IVA.28 *Church, State, and Society in Eastern Europe: Hungarian Philosophical Studies, I.* Miklós Tomka. ISBN 156518226X (paper).
IVA.29 *Politics, Ethics, and the Challenges to Democracy in 'New Independent States': Georgian Philosophical Studies, II.* Tinatin Bochorishvili, William Sweet, Daniel Ahern, eds. ISBN 9781565182240 (paper).
IVA.30 *Comparative Ethics in a Global Age: Russian Philosophical Studies II.* Marietta T. Stepanyants, eds. ISBN 9781565182356 (paper).
IVA.31 *Identity and Values of Lithuanians: Lithuanian Philosophical Studies, V.* Aida Savicka, eds. ISBN 9781565182367 (paper).
IVA.32 *The Challenge of Our Hope: Christian Faith in Dialogue: Polish Philosophical Studies, VII.* Waclaw Hryniewicz. ISBN 9781565182370 (paper).
IVA.33 *Diversity and Dialogue: Culture and Values in the Age of Globalization.* Andrew Blasko and Plamen Makariev, eds. ISBN 9781565182387 (paper).
IVA. 34 *Civil Society, Pluralism and Universalism: Polish Philosophical Studies, VIII.* Eugeniusz Gorski. ISBN 9781565182417 (paper).
IVA.35 *Romanian Philosophical Culture, Globalization, and Education*: *Romanian Philosophical Studies VI.* Stefan Popenici and Alin Tat and, eds. ISBN 9781565182424 (paper).
IVA.36 *Political Transformation and Changing Identities in Central and Eastern Europe: Lithuanian Philosophical Studies, VI.* Andrew Blasko and Diana Janušauskienė, eds. ISBN 9781565182462 (paper).
IVA.37 *Truth and Morality: The Role of Truth in Public Life: Romanian Philosophical Studies, VII.* Wilhelm Dancă, ed. ISBN 9781565182493 (paper).
IVA.38 *Globalization and Culture: Outlines of Contemporary Social Cognition: Lithuanian Philosophical Studies, VII.* Jurate Morkuniene, ed. ISBN 9781565182516 (paper).
IVA.39 *Knowledge and Belief in the Dialogue of Cultures*, *Russian Philosophical Studies, III.* Marietta Stepanyants, ed. ISBN 9781565182622 (paper).
IVA.40 *God and the Post-Modern Thought: Philosophical Issues in the Contemporary Critique of Modernity, Polish Philosophical Studies, IX.* Józef Życiński. ISBN 9781565182677 (paper).

IVA.41 *Dialogue among Civilizations, Russian Philosophical Studies, IV.* Nur Kirabaev and Yuriy Pochta, eds. ISBN 9781565182653 (paper).

IVA.42 *The Idea of Solidarity: Philosophical and Social Contexts, Polish Philosophical Studies, X.* Dariusz Dobrzanski, ed. ISBN 9781565182961 (paper).

IVA.43 *God's Spirit in the World: Ecumenical and Cultural Essays, Polish Philosophical Studies, XI.* Waclaw Hryniewicz. ISBN 9781565182738 (paper).

IVA.44 *Philosophical Theology and the Christian Traditions: Russian and Western Perspectives, Russian Philosophical Studies, V.* David Bradshaw, ed. ISBN 9781565182752 (paper).

IVA.45 *Ethics and the Challenge of Secularism: Russian Philosophical Studies, VI.* David Bradshaw, ed. ISBN 9781565182806 (paper).

IVA.46 *Philosophy and Spirituality across Cultures and Civilizations: Russian Philosophical Studies, VII.* Nur Kirabaev, Yuriy Pochta and Ruzana Pskhu, eds. ISBN 9781565182820 (paper).

IVA.47 *Values of the Human Person Contemporary Challenges: Romanian Philosophical Studies, VIII.* Mihaela Pop, ed. ISBN 9781565182844 (paper).

IVA.48 *Faith and Secularization: A Romanian Narrative: Romanian Philosophical Studies, IX.* Wilhelm Dancă, ed. ISBN 9781565182929 (paper).

IVA.49 *The Spirit: The Cry of the World: Polish Philosophical Studies, XII.* Waclaw Hryniewicz. ISBN 9781565182943 (paper).

IVA.50 *Philosophy and Science in Cultures: East and West: Russian Philosophical Studies, VIII.* Marietta T. Stepanyants, ed. ISBN 9781565182967 (paper).

IVA.51 *A Czech Perspective on Faith in a Secular Age: Czech Philosophical Studies V.* Tomáš Halík and Pavel Hošek, eds. ISBN 9781565183001 (paper).

IVA52 *Dilemmas of the Catholic Church in Poland: Polish Philosophical Studies, XIII.* Tadeusz Buksinski, ed. ISBN 9781565183025 (paper).

IVA53 *Secularization and Intensification of Religion in Modern Society: Polish Philosophical Studies, XIV.* Leon Dyczewski, ed. ISBN 9781565183032 (paper).

IVA54 *Seekers or Dweller: The Social Character of Religion in Hungary: Hungarian Philosophical Studies, II.* Zsuzsanna Bögre, ed. ISBN9781565183063 (paper).

Series V. Latin American Philosophical Studies

V.1 *The Social Context and Values: Perspectives of the Americas.* O. Pegoraro, ed. ISBN 081917355X (paper); 0819173541 (cloth).

V.2 *Culture, Human Rights and Peace in Central America.* Raul Molina and Timothy Ready, eds. ISBN 0819173576 (paper); 0819173568 (cloth).

V.3 *El Cristianismo Aymara: Inculturacion o Culturizacion?* Luis Jolicoeur. ISBN 1565181042 (paper).
V.4 *Love as the Foundation of Moral Education and Character Development.* Luis Ugalde, Nicolas Barros and George F. McLean, eds. ISBN 1565180801 (paper).
V.5 *Human Rights, Solidarity and Subsidiarity: Essays towards a Social Ontology.* Carlos E.A. Maldonado. ISBN 1565181107 (paper).
V.6 *A New World: A Perspective from Ibero America.* H. Daniel Dei, ed. ISBN 9781565182639 (paper).

Series VI. Foundations of Moral Education

VI.1 *Philosophical Foundations for Moral Education and Character Development: Act and Agent.* G. McLean and F. Ellrod, eds. ISBN 156518001-1 (paper); ISBN 1565180003 (cloth).
VI.2 *Psychological Foundations for Moral Education and Character Development: An Integrated Theory of Moral Development.* R. Knowles, ed. ISBN 156518002X (paper); 156518003-8 (cloth).
VI.3 *Character Development in Schools and Beyond.* Kevin Ryan and Thomas Lickona, eds. ISBN 1565180593 (paper); 156518058-5 (cloth).
VI.4 *The Social Context and Values: Perspectives of the Americas.* O. Pegoraro, ed. ISBN 081917355X (paper); 0819173541 (cloth).
VI.5 *Chinese Foundations for Moral Education and Character Development.* Tran van Doan, ed. ISBN 1565180321 (paper); 156518033 (cloth).
VI.6 *Love as the Foundation of Moral Education and Character Development.* Luis Ugalde, Nicolas Barros and George F. McLean, eds. ISBN 1565180801 (paper).

Series VII. Seminars on Culture and Values

VII.1 *The Social Context and Values: Perspectives of the Americas.* O. Pegoraro, ed. ISBN 081917355X (paper); 0819173541 (cloth).
VII.2 *Culture, Human Rights and Peace in Central America.* Raul Molina and Timothy Ready, eds. ISBN 0819173576 (paper); 0819173568 (cloth).
VII.3 *Relations between Cultures.* John A. Kromkowski, ed. ISBN 1565180089 (paper); 1565180097 (cloth).
VII.4 *Moral Imagination and Character Development: Volume I, The Imagination.* George F. McLean and John A. Kromkowski, eds. ISBN 1565181743 (paper).
VII.5 *Moral Imagination and Character Development: Volume II, Moral Imagination in Personal Formation and Character Development.* George F. McLean and Richard Knowles, eds. ISBN 1565181816 (paper).

VII.6 *Moral Imagination and Character Development: Volume III, Imagination in Religion and Social Life*. George F. McLean and John K. White, eds. ISBN 1565181824 (paper).
VII.7 *Hermeneutics and Inculturation*. George F. McLean, Antonio Gallo, Robert Magliola, eds. ISBN 1565181840 (paper).
VII.8 *Culture, Evangelization, and Dialogue*. Antonio Gallo and Robert Magliola, eds. ISBN 1565181832 (paper).
VII.9 *The Place of the Person in Social Life*. Paul Peachey and John A. Kromkowski, eds. ISBN 1565180127 (paper); 156518013-5 (cloth).
VII.10 *Urbanization and Values*. John A. Kromkowski, ed. ISBN 1565180100 (paper); 1565180119 (cloth).
VII.11 *Freedom and Choice in a Democracy, Volume I: Meanings of Freedom*. Robert Magliola and John Farrelly, eds. ISBN 1565181867 (paper).
VII.12 *Freedom and Choice in a Democracy, Volume II: The Difficult Passage to Freedom*. Robert Magliola and Richard Khuri, eds. ISBN 1565181859 (paper).
VII 13 *Cultural Identity, Pluralism and Globalization* (2 volumes). John P. Hogan, ed. ISBN 1565182170 (paper).
VII.14 *Democracy: In the Throes of Liberalism and Totalitarianism*. George F. McLean, Robert Magliola, William Fox, eds. ISBN 1565181956 (paper).
VII.15 *Democracy and Values in Global Times: With Nigeria as a Case Study*. George F. McLean, Robert Magliola, Joseph Abah, eds. ISBN 1565181956 (paper).
VII.16 *Civil Society and Social Reconstruction*. George F. McLean, ed. ISBN 1565180860 (paper).
VII.17 *Civil Society: Who Belongs?* William A.Barbieri, Robert Magliola, Rosemary Winslow, eds. ISBN 1565181972 (paper).
VII.18 *The Humanization of Social Life: Theory and Challenges*. Christopher Wheatley, Robert P. Badillo, Rose B. Calabretta, Robert Magliola, eds. ISBN 1565182006 (paper).
VII.19 *The Humanization of Social Life: Cultural Resources and Historical Responses*. Ronald S. Calinger, Robert P. Badillo, Rose B. Calabretta, Robert Magliola, eds. ISBN 1565182006 (paper).
VII.20 *Religious Inspiration for Public Life: Religion in Public Life, Volume I*. George F. McLean, John A. Kromkowski and Robert Magliola, eds. ISBN 1565182103 (paper).
VII.21 *Religion and Political Structures from Fundamentalism to Public Service: Religion in Public Life, Volume II*. John T. Ford, Robert A. Destro and Charles R. Dechert, eds. ISBN 1565182111 (paper).
VII.22 *Civil Society as Democratic Practice*. Antonio F. Perez, Semou Pathé Gueye, Yang Fenggang, eds. ISBN 1565182146 (paper).
VII.23 *Ecumenism and Nostra Aetate in the 21st Century*. George F. McLean and John P. Hogan, eds. ISBN 1565182197 (paper).

VII.24 *Multiple Paths to God: Nostra Aetate: 40 years Later.* John P. Hogan, George F. McLean & John A. Kromkowski, eds. ISBN 1565182200 (paper).
VII.25 *Globalization and Identity.* Andrew Blasko, Taras Dobko, Pham Van Duc and George Pattery, eds. ISBN 1565182200 (paper).
VII.26 *Communication across Cultures: The Hermeneutics of Cultures and Religions in a Global Age.* Chibueze C. Udeani, Veerachart Nimanong, Zou Shipeng, Mustafa Malik, eds. ISBN: 9781565182400 (paper).
VII.27 *Symbols, Cultures and Identities in a Time of Global Interaction.* Paata Chkheidze, Hoang Thi Tho and Yaroslav Pasko, eds. ISBN 9781565182608 (paper).
VII. 28 *Restorying the 'Polis':Civil Society as Narrative Reconstruction.* Yuriy Pochta, Rosemary Winslow, eds. ISNB 978156518 (paper).
VII.29 *History and Cultural Identity: Retrieving the Past, Shaping the Future.* John P. Hogan, ed. ISBN 9781565182684 (paper).
VII.30 *Human Nature: Stable and/or Changing?* John P. Hogan, ed. ISBN 9781565182431 (paper).
VII.31 *Reasoning in Faith: Cultural Foundations for Civil Society and Globalization.* Octave Kamwiziku Wozol, Sebastian Velassery and Jurate Baranova, eds. ISBN 9781565182868 (paper).
VII.32 *Building Community in a Mobile/Global Age: Migration and Hospitality.* John P. Hogan, Vensus A. George and Corazon T. Toralba, eds. ISBN 9781565182875 (paper).
VII.33 *The Role of Religions in the Public-Sphere: The Post-Secular Model of Jürgen Habermas and Beyond.* Plamen Makariev and Vensus A. George, eds. ISBN 9781565183049 (paper).

Series VIII. Christian Philosophical Studies

VIII.1 *Church and People: Disjunctions in a Secular Age, Christian Philosophical Studies, I.* Charles Taylor, José Casanova and George F. McLean, eds. ISBN9781565182745 (paper).
VIII.2 *God's Spirit in the World: Ecumenical and Cultural Essays, Christian Philosophical Studies, II.* Waclaw Hryniewicz. ISBN 9781565182738 (paper).
VIII.3 *Philosophical Theology and the Christian Traditions: Russian and Western Perspectives, Christian Philosophical Studies, III.* David Bradshaw, ed. ISBN 9781565182752 (paper).
VIII.4 *Ethics and the Challenge of Secularism: Christian Philosophical Studies, IV.* David Bradshaw, ed. ISBN 9781565182806 (paper).
VIII.5 *Freedom for Faith: Theological Hermeneutics of Discovery based on George F. McLean's Philosophy of Culture: Christian Philosophical Studies, V.* John M. Staak. ISBN 9781565182837 (paper).

VIII.6 *Humanity on the Threshold: Religious Perspective on Transhumanism: Christian Philosophical Studies, VI.* John C. Haughey and Ilia Delio, eds. ISBN 9781565182882 (paper).
VIII.7 *Faith and Secularization: A Romanian Narrative: Christian Philosophical Studies, VII.* Wilhelm Dancă, ed. ISBN 9781565182929 (paper).
VIII.8 *Towards a Kenotic Vision of Authority in the Catholic Church: Christian Philosophical Studies, VIII.* Anthony J. Carroll, Marthe Kerkwijk, Michael Kirwan and James Sweeney, eds. ISBN 9781565182936 (paper).
VIII.9 *The Spirit: The Cry of the World: Christian Philosophical Studies, IX.* Waclaw Hryniewicz. ISBN 9781565182943 (paper).
VIII.10 *A Czech Perspective on Faith in a Secular Age: Christian Philosophical Studies, X.* Tomáš Halík and Pavel Hošek, eds. ISBN 9781565183001 (paper).
VIII.11 *A Catholic Minority Church in a World of Seekers: Christian Philosophical Studies, XI.* Staf Hellemans and Peter Jonkers, eds. ISBN 9781565183018 (paper).
VIII.12 *Dilemmas of the Catholic Church in Poland: Christian Philosophical Studies, XII.* Tadeusz Buksinski, ed. ISBN 9781565183025 (paper).
VIII.13 *Secularization and Intensification of Religion in Modern Society: Christian Philosophical Studies, XIII.* Leon Dyczewski, ed. ISBN 9781565183032 (paper).
VIII.14 *Plural Spiritualities: North American Experience: Christian Philosophical Studies, XIV.* Robert J. Schreiter, ed. ISBN 9781565183056 (paper).
VIII.15 *Seekers or Dwellers: The Social Character of Religion in Hungary: Christian Philosophical Studies, XV.* Zsuzsanna Bögre, ed. ISBN 9781565183063 (paper).

The International Society for Metaphysics

ISM.1 *Person and Nature.* George F. McLean and Hugo Meynell, eds. ISBN 0819170267 (paper); 0819170259 (cloth).
ISM.2 *Person and Society.* George F. McLean and Hugo Meynell, eds. ISBN 0819169250 (paper); 0819169242 (cloth).
ISM.3 *Person and God.* George F. McLean and Hugo Meynell, eds. ISBN 0819169382 (paper); 0819169374 (cloth).
ISM.4 *The Nature of Metaphysical Knowledge.* George F. McLean and Hugo Meynell, eds. ISBN 0819169277 (paper); 0819169269 (cloth).
ISM.5 *Philosophhical Challenges and Opportunities of Globalization.* Oliva Blanchette, Tomonobu Imamichi and George F. McLean, eds. ISBN 1565181298 (paper).

ISM.6 *The Dialogue of Cultural Traditions: Global Perspective.* William Sweet, George F. McLean, Tomonobu Imamichi, Safak Ural, O. Faruk Akyol, eds. ISBN 9781565182585 (paper).

ISM. 7 *Philosophy Emerging from Culture.* William Sweet, George F. McLean, Oliva Blanchette, Wonbin Park, eds. ISBN 9781565182851 (paper).

The series is published by: The Council for Research in Values and Philosophy, Gibbons Hall B-20, 620 Michigan Avenue, NE, Washington, D.C. 20064; Telephone and Fax: 202/319-6089; e-mail: cua-rvp@cua.edu; website: http://www.crvp.org. All titles are available in paper except as noted.

The series is distributed by: The Council for Research on Values and Philosophy – OST, 285 Oblate Drive, San Antonio, T.X., 78216; Telephone: (210)341-1366 x205; Email: mmartin@ost.edu.